The fate of the Sleeping Beauties

We dedicate this book to Andrea, Louise, Madeleine, Marlous, Nils and Ronja.

Only the support and understanding of our loved ones has enabled us to spend so many evenings and weekends working towards our dream of putting this book together step by step. Thank you all!

Arnoud, Ard and Kay

Other great books from Veloce –

Those Were The Days ... Series
American 'Independent' Automakers – AMC to Willys 1945 to 1960 (Mort)
American Station Wagons – The Golden Era 1950-1975 (Mort)
American Woodies 1928-1953 (Mort)
Anglo-American Cars from the 1930s to the 1970s (Mort)
Austerity Motoring (Bobbitt)
Austins, The last real (Peck)
British Woodies (Peck)
Last Real Austins 1946-1959, The (Peck)

General
Armstrong-Siddeley (Smith)
Bentley Continental, Corniche & Azure (Bennett)
Bentley MkVI, R & S/R-R Silver Wraith, Dawn & Cloud (Nutland)
British Cars, The Complete Catalogue of, 1895-1975 (Culshaw & Horrobin)
Bugatti Type 40 (Price)
Bugatti 46/50 Updated Edition (Price & Arbey)
Bugatti T44 & T49 (Price & Arbey)
Bugatti 57 2nd Edition (Price)
Citroën DS (Bobbitt)
East German Motor Vehicles in Pictures (Suhr/Weinreich)
Jaguar, The Rise of (Price)
Rolls-Royce Silver Shadow/Bentley T-Series (Bobbitt)
Rolls-Royce Silver Spirit, Silver Spur & Bentley Mulsanne (Bobbitt)
Singer Story: Cars, Commercial Vehicles, Bicycles & Motorcycles (Atkinson)
Sleeping Beauties USA – abandoned classic cars & trucks (Marek)

From Veloce Publishing's new imprints:

Battle Cry!
Soviet General & field rank officer uniforms: 1955 to 1991 (Streather)
Red & Soviet military & paramilitary services: female uniforms 1941-1991 (Streather)

Hubble & Hattie
Clever Dog! (O'Meara)
Complete Dog Massage Manual, The – Gentle Dog Care (Robertson)
Dinner with Rover (Paton-Ayre)
Dog Cookies (Schops/Pick)
Dog Games – Stimulating play to entertain your dog and you (Blenski)
Dog Relax – Relaxed dogs, relaxed owners (Pilguj)
Exercising your puppy: a gentle & natural approach (Robertson/Pope)
Know Your Dog – The guide to a beautiful relationship (Birmelin)
Living with an Older Dog (Alderton/Hall)
My dog is blind – but lives life to the full! (Horsky)
Smellorama – nose games for dogs (Theby)
Waggy Tails & Wheelchairs (Epp)
Walkin' the dog – motorway walks for drivers and dogs (Rees)
Winston ... the dog who changed my life (Klute)
You and Your Border Terrier – The Essential Guide (Alderton)
You and Your Cockapoo – The Essential Guide (Alderton)

www.veloce.co.uk

First published in English October 2010 by Veloce Publishing Limited, Veloce House, Parkway Farm Business Park, Middle Farm Way, Poundbury, Dorchester, Dorset, DT1 3AR, England. Originally published in 2008 as "Het lot van de Slapende Schoonheden" by Uitgeverij de Alk BV.
Fax 01305 250479/e-mail info@veloce.co.uk/web www.veloce.co.uk or www.velocebooks.com.

ISBN: 978-1-845840-70-9 UPC: 6-36847-04070-3

Readers with ideas for automotive books, or books on other transport or related hobby subjects, are invited to write to the editorial director of Veloce Publishing at the above address.
British Library Cataloguing in Publication Data – A catalogue record for this book is available from the British Library.
Typesetting, design and page make-up all by Veloce Publishing Ltd on Apple Mac. Printed in India by Replika Press.

Ard op de Weegh – Kay Hottendorff – Arnoud op de Weegh

The fate of the

Sleeping Beauties

VELOCE PUBLISHING
THE PUBLISHER OF FINE AUTOMOTIVE BOOKS

Contents

CRSO

Publisher's note

Throughout the text of this book the reader will find small numbers in superscript, these numbers relate to the
bibliography to be found on page 150.

Foreword by Michel Dovaz

❦

I really don't enjoy talking about the past and find the present and future much more interesting. This is probably because recalling the past reminds us of things we haven't done and things we regret.

In late 2007, however, I had occasion to discuss the past when I met up with Ard and Arnoud op de Weegh and Kay Hottendorff. Obviously the subject of conversation was old cars, and more specifically Bugattis.

There are three reasons why I have avoided this subject for so long.

Firstly, there aren't many people around who can imagine what it was like in the past. For instance, if you talk about cars and the 1950s to someone who has not experienced that period, you soon come across as a dreamer or an eccentric who has let slip an opportunity.

Just imagine the mood of the times. Shortly after the war there was no problem in getting hold of a Hispano-Suiza, a Delage D8, a Bugatti or a Mercedes 540K, the difficulty was getting rid of them. And it was not just a question of price. Hardly anybody wanted the cars because of their high petrol consumption. Placing an advertisement in the newspaper was a complete waste of money. That's why so many cars, especially large, petrol-slurping models, ended up on the scrapheap.

I know what I am talking about, as well: On one occasion I went to the Pershing garage in the boulevard Pershing in Paris to look over a Hispano twelve-cylinder, two-seater cabriolet, a beautiful car,

in immaculate condition, on sale at a modest price. While I was examining the car a salesman, seeing my interest, approached me and said: "We have two twelve-cylinder models for sale. If you take both, I'll give you the second for half-price." But I didn't buy them because of the petrol consumption!

Another example: a certain Rioux, a great stockcars amateur, raced with twelve-cylinder engines. Due to the enormous torque he left everyone standing at the start. But not long afterwards the whole scene came to an end as these cars had spoked wheels and were therefore very frail. They ended up on the scrapheap.

Secondly I also ask myself where all the so-called 'enthusiasts' were at this time (ie those who now make a round trip of 50 kilometres in order to buy a 8mm collar bolt) when scrap merchants were using oxyacetylene cutters to slice 35Bs, 55s, or even worse, Type 50s, into pieces. In those days, cars were worth no more than their weight. The heavier they were the more valuable they were, at least for a scrap merchant. There was a surcharge for aluminium and Bugattis were the only French cars which incorporated a large amount of aluminium.

Thirdly there is the question of 'value'. On the one hand, many people have suddenly become interested in classic cars because they are money-spinners. In a prosperous society, where camembert boxes and coat hangers are objects worthy of collection and everything old is avidly sought after, why not cars? On the other hand, everything that is expensive or wealthy is coming into prominence, whether it's a Van Gogh, a bottle of Château Lafite 1811, a well-known singer, footballer or racing driver. The sums involved arouse interest in objects and people that under normal circumstances would not mean anything to anybody. Nuvolari, an extraordinary racing driver, who was very poorly paid, was more or less anonymous, while Schumacher, who is 'worth' 500 million euros per year, is a legend. And once a car becomes a collectors' item, then a murderous competition arises amongst 'enthusiasts' for cars that are worthy, or not, of attention. It is a question of who has the most beautiful, the most unusual and the most expensive, with the owner taking all the acclaim and not the car.

For the above and other reasons, I have avoided the subject, in particular since my career took a different course in this respect, but now I am ready to look back at the 1950s.

At that time I bought my first Bugatti at Teillac, a large Bugatti garage in the avenue de Suffren, nearly

Michel Dovaz in 2007. (Hottendorff/op de Weegh)

opposite the current UNESCO building. The Bugatti make was a bit shaky on its feet, but if you ordered a part from the factory you normally received it. On the other hand, everyone was waiting for the new model, which was indeed a long time coming.

The Bugatti garage was actually a large hall. The cars for sale were lined up to the left and right of a central corridor and at the back, in a separate area, were the workshops. In the hall stood about twenty Bugattis, ranging from a 2.3-litre supercharged model to a 57C. Due to the fact that it had four seats I actually wanted a 57, but hadn't got the necessary cash. I therefore bought a grey 49 cabriolet, with a blue leather interior. I seem to remember the car had been owned by Jean-Luc Michelin who had part-exchanged it for a 57, in which he later had a fatal accident on the way to Clermont-Ferrand.

I paid 135,000 (old) French francs and went to the headquarters of the Paris police to have the *carte grise* (French vehicle registration document) changed. The procedure consisted of signing a printed form which stated that 'the car had not been modified and was fitted with a rear-view mirror' and then paying 32 francs.

In the evening, I set off for Geneva with a spare jerry can of petrol, as Bugattis had a reputation for being heavy on fuel (which incidentally is untrue) and there wasn't a single petrol station open en route, except in Dijon, which was 520km away. After I had refuelled in Dijon I was a confirmed *Bugattiste*, a member of a sort of secret brotherhood, who greeted each other when their paths crossed, but also because like every Bugatti owner I had suffered from unavoidable engine problems. These problems were unavoidable, because the original head gaskets were aluminium and very prone to corrosion. Later they were replaced by copper gaskets, but the factory should have thought about that in the first place.

The rear axle also was too lightly constructed. It was perfectly okay for the 44, but regularly went wrong on the 49 and failed completely on the 57. Eventually the factory found the fault and fitted a heavier axle.

In addition, the crankshaft was loaded at one end by the camshaft drive and the supercharger drive and at the other end by the traction, which meant a torsion arose that subjected the crankshaft to a considerable force. It was predominantly a fault on the Type 50; on the Type 57 it was redressed and on the Alfa Romeo it did not normally occur.

But there was another side to all these deficiencies as the following short tale, typical of the 1950s, illustrates.

One Saturday, accompanied by my brother, I took the 49 to pick up a 'stateless' journalist friend in the XII arrondissement. For convenience we shall call him 'Alain'. We all went away for the weekend, which wasn't so common in those days. At the time there was a short section of motorway from Paris to Versailles, about twenty kilometres long, known as the 'Autoroute de l'Ouest'. Here we gave the car its head and pressed the accelerator pedal to the floor. Near the Palace of Versailles, Alain, who was sitting in the back, said that there was a smell of burning and then that he could see smoke. We stopped to investigate. The smoke was coming from the back seat. I lifted the seat up and saw that it was on fire. We quickly doused the flames and noticed that the cause appeared to be a seat spring that had been pressed down against the drive shaft (there was no dividing panel between the rear seat and the chassis). We re-secured the spring and carried on with our journey.

A few months later, in the early morning, Alain was apprehended by the 'DST', a sort of internal security service. He was considered to be a spy and was therefore followed 24 hours a day. Alain was interrogated. They knew everything about him, except what he had been doing on a certain Saturday, when the police, who drove the well-known Citroën Traction Avant cars, had lost sight of him. Tractions of course were only capable of 115 kilometres per hour (on the speedometer) and the Bugatti Type 49, which was then twenty years old, could easily exceed 140kph. A 57C could even reach 180kph!

I wasn't able to sell the first cars I bought. The only choice was to take them to the breakers – which in fact I sometimes had to do – or to keep them, which was not easy if you had no suitable storage area. At that time I used to go regularly to look at a Duesenberg near Porte de Vincennes, where there were many secondhand dealers. Years later the motoring journalist and collecter Serge Pozzoli told me that he also had often examined this strange two-seater with aluminium engine block and bodywork. On the cowling there was a panel with many Bugatti patents. The car had almost certainly been the property of the circus owner Médrano. I really wanted to have the Duesenberg, but when I had finally solved the storage problem, aluminium prices had shot up due to the Vietnam war. The dealer, who left the unsaleable car out in the open, had meanwhile sold it to a scrap merchant!

Having retained a reasonable number of cars, always with the idea of driving a specific model again, perhaps after a few small repairs, I did not sell them when fashions changed and prices rose. Not only because I didn't want to encourage the prevailing madness, but also because they were inextricably linked to many memories and to many problems that had only been solved with great difficulty. Cars are heavy, large, and difficult to move, and there were many more problems of this kind. During the last move, from Seine et Marne to Quercy, a distance of 650 kilometres, we had to transport 70 vehicles, a task, nay an ordeal, that I wouldn't wish on anybody.

The following pages, which reflect the painstaking work undertaken by the authors, testify to the salvation of many cars that would otherwise have disappeared completely.

Michel Dovaz

Acknowledgements

ভঙ্ক

Without the incredible amount of support we received from numerous classic car enthusiasts, car crazy folk, marque experts, participants in Internet forums and car owners, we would have never been able to finish this book. Many of them added valuable pieces to our puzzle, and some even joined us with great enthusiasm as we put it all together. Due to the large number of contacts, we sometimes couldn't see the wood for the trees so please don't be offended if you're not included in the list below. We would particularly like to thank the following:

Jean-Claude Anaf, Toine Bakx & Valerie Blanchard, Corrado Bellabarba, Henrik Betnér, Boudewijn Berkhoff, Fritz Berger, Dorien Berteletti, Cédric Billequé, John de Boer, Vic Brincat, Hermann Brouwer, Chris Brown, Johan Buchner, Jonathan Cence, John Chamberlain, Dennis Coleman, Luc Colemont, Edvar van Daalen, Lionel Decrey, Gilles Delannoy, Dominique Delcros, Andre Dufilho, Patrick Faucompre, Tim Fritz, Thierry Giovannoni, Nicolas Guhring, Bernhard Graf-Saner, Christoph Grohe, Francesco Guasti, Florian Handlbauer, Herbert Handlbauer, Helge Hauk, Douwe Heida, Kevin Herron, Jaap Horst, Michael Hortig, Harry Hoving, Kees Jansen, Dick Janssen, Rick Jones, J Michael Jordan, Martijn Kaman, Wilfried Kruse, Julius Kruta, Didier Lainé, Victor Lane, Pierre Yves Laugier, Carlo Laven, André Lecoq, Haje van der Leer, Dirk Libeert, Roger Lund, Michael T Lynch, Josh B Malks, Peter Marshall, M Tyler Mathis, Theo Meinster, Gerrit Mobach, Edmund Nankivell, Jan-Peter Neelsen, Hildegard Nesswetter, Philippe Ogier, Dennis Ortenburger, Bertrand de Passemar, Michel Pfau, Norbert Pipper, Benoit Prick Jr., Jean Prick, Urs-Paul Ramseier, Jonathan Richards, Jonathan Rishton, Jaap Braam Ruben, David Saunders, Roland Saunier, Björn Schmidt, Henk Scholten Volvo, Bernhard Simon, David B Smith, Maurice Soutif, Jan Spiele, Jan Stockhusen, Danielle Tarrade, Michel de Thomasson, Daniel Turpin, Yan Verdier, Michel Villard, Niek Versteeg, Patrick Vervuuren, Martijn Visser, Uwe Wießmath and Martin van der Zeeuw as well as the current owners of the Bugattis with chassis numbers 44580, 49410, 50113 and 55233.

Of course, we would like to extend our very special thanks to Michel Dovaz, without whose passion for and fascination with cars the subject of this book would probably have been put on the scrap heap decades ago. It was the active support we received from him that enabled us to create a book that is so much more authentic than anything we could have done on our own.

Besides these and many other helpful people, we also ran into some who consistently ignored us and a few who even tried to actively undermine our efforts. For obvious reasons we will not name names in this book but we would like to thank them anyway. After all, their conduct kept our fighting spirit alive and was ultimately very helpful in enabling us to finish this book successfully.

9

The history of the sleeping beauties

Prologue:
Three men in search of the truth

ca⬡so

In 1997 the wife-to-be of Kay Hottendorff, a German engineer living near Hamburg, presented him with a poster showing a prominent image of a Bugatti Ventoux taken from the front of a book entitled *Sleeping Beauties* [1] published in 1986 by Herbert Hesselmann and Halwart Schrader.

The book comprises photographs of a collection of neglected classic cars, including various Bugattis, which Hesselmann came across on a farm in France in 1983.

Kay, who was very interested in the history of cars, was fascinated by the faded beauty of the car on the poster and by the Bugatti make. This prompted him to set about searching on the internet and via various forums for clues that would enable him to find out more about the collection of 'Pierre', as mentioned in the book. Kay had the same questions that taxed everyone who read the book from the 1980s: Where is the collection? Who is the mysterious owner? How could decay have gone so far? Were the cars ever sold or even restored?

By spending thousands of hours searching on the internet and by communicating with other car enthusiasts on forums, Kay was able to gather a remarkable amount of information over a period of many years. However, a host of questions still remained unanswered. Kay was especially pre-occupied with the fate of the collection and the motives of the owner.

In 2001, Ard op de Weegh, director of two primary schools in Arnhem, was given the *Sleeping Beauties*

book by his colleague, Tristan Veneman. Because they were both out-and-out car enthusiasts, they regularly discussed the book. Shortly afterwards, however, destiny intervened and Tristan become terminally ill. Ard visited him regularly, and on these occasions they often discussed profound questions of life and death, but naturally also their common hobby. In June 2002 Tristan revealed that if his time on earth had permitted, he would have set about searching for the collection. This statement ie the fact that he wouldn't be able to undertake any more projects because his life was coming to an end, made a deep impression on Ard. Later, Tristan gave Ard a pile of French and Dutch magazines which contained a mass of supplementary information.

Tristan died shortly before Christmas 2002. At the funeral Ard heard Tristan's partner, Marlène, relate how passionate he was about cars, so Ard decided to turn his life upside down for the foreseeable future: "I will look for the cars, and I will find them." he proclaimed.

Arnoud op de Weegh, an automotive engineering student, often saw his father leafing through books and spending hours scanning magazines. Ard explained that he was searching for clues that would put him on the track of the collection, part of which was last seen in a museum in Sarlat (the museum closed in 1990).

Arnoud began surfing the net, but what he found was not very encouraging. Many people had tried to trace the collection but, apart from a single vehicle,

Kay Hottendorff in 2008 with poster and the book from which it derived; both show the image which has fascinated him since 1997. (Hottendorff/op de Weegh)

nobody had unearthed anything. All search attempts came to a dead end and were therefore abandoned. The mysterious owner had gone to ground and could not be found anywhere.

Arnoud then suggested that he and his father should visit Sarlat, as it was there that the last traces of the collection were recorded. In the summer of 2006 the two men set off for France where they unearthed a great deal of interesting information; information which they took back home and classified whilst continuing the search.

So, at the end of 2006, two Dutchmen and a German were busy searching for information about the fate of the 'sleeping beauties,' completely unaware of each other's quest. They had many contacts, but most of them provided little or no information. However, the independently assembled

Ard (left) and Arnoud op de Weegh in 2007 with the restored Bugatti from the poster, a 1935 Type 57 Ventoux. (Hottendorff/op de Weegh)

Arnoud op de Weegh with the Cord 812 at Château de Sanxet, 2007.
(Hottendorff/op de Weegh)

piles of information continued to grow steadily. In December 2006, Arnoud alerted his father to a member of a car forum, who was asking many pertinent questions about the collection.

Ard emailed the person who turned out to be Kay Hottendorff. From the exchange of emails, it seemed that Kay was somebody who had valuable and detailed information so, on Boxing Day, Ard and Arnoud decided to drive to Germany to meet the man and find out what sort of person he was. Kay in turn had the same idea. After a rather cautious introduction, the three men decided to cooperate and proceed with the project. This turned out to be a very good decision indeed ...

Take the down-to-earth and businesslike Kay (born 1969), who can sit at his computer for hours, patiently searching for information, making contact by email and classifying the resulting

information. Then there is Arnoud (born 1988), who immerses himself in the technical aspects of the subject, an indispensable sparring partner for his father, continually monitoring the business and material aspects of the project that arise from their discussions. And, finally, the perceptive Ard (born 1952), whose competence in English, French and German means that he is constantly making new contacts and conversing with people all over the world. Kay's work is based on facts and logical connections, Arnoud sticks to the straight and narrow and searches tenaciously, while Ard is a people person, preferring to work with empathy and intuition. In short, three men from different generations with very different qualities, who complement each other perfectly.

This book documents the remarkable results of this cross-border and cross-generation cooperation.

Cars under dust

∞

In 1983, the classic car world was shaken by a series of articles in the international press. A German photographer, Herbert Hesselmann, published photos of a collection of priceless classic cars, languishing in a 19th century farmyard in the hamlet of Villemaréchal, about 100 kilometres south of Paris.

The pictures of the cars, under a thick coating of dust, caused many enthusiasts to react in horror. Hesselmann highlighted the fact that here, more than fifty top-quality cars, including unique Bugattis, were returning to a 'state of nature.' He underlined this situation with photographic perfection. It aroused many emotions, and the photos were promptly sold to many international magazines. Then in 1986, a book appeared, which was published in three languages.

The owner of the collection had been put in touch with the photographer, by a friend named Guido Bartolomeo. After much urging, Hesselmann and Bartolomeo were able to persuade the owner, Michel Dovaz, to allow them to take photos for the sum of DM 2000. Dovaz permitted this, on the express condition that neither his name, nor the location of the cars, appeared in any of the publications. In addition, there were to be no photos of him, or the outer walls of the farm. This was because car parts had been stolen on occasions, and he didn't want large amounts of publicity about the collection. Dovaz also reached an agreement with Hesselmann that the photos would be published in Germany only, and certainly not in France. Consequently, when a damning article appeared in the French magazine,

Geo, Dovaz started legal proceedings against it, and won. A spate of condemnatory articles about his collection appeared in publications around the world. Michel ignored them, and to this day does not want to read anything more about the publications, nor see Hesselmann's book.

Hesselmann agreed with the conditions, and was able to work for a few days undisturbed, whilst enjoying Dovaz's generous hospitality. When Hesselmann and his team had finished, Dovaz organised a dinner for his German guests, and opened fourteen bottles of expensive wine to celebrate the successful outcome of the project. On balance, the celebration had cost Dovaz more than the sum he had received for the photographic session.

The photographer felt instinctively that the pictures and the story he had prepared was something very special. He approached several magazine publishers, but was met with universal disbelief. The general feeling was that it was not possible for so many valuable cars to be languishing in one place. But, to back up his assertion, Hesselmann had made a sixteen minute video film, which meant that the publishers had no choice but to accept the story behind the photos; and it was not long before these appeared in publications throughout the world.

In September 1983, the German magazine *Stern* published a comprehensive article about the collection, illustrated with many photos. In the accompanying text, written by Walther Wuttke, Michel Dovaz was pulled to pieces. He was

The famous barn which hosted three Bugattis, two Cords, and one Alfa Romeo back in 1983. Nothing reminds of them in 2009. (Courtesy Kevin Herron)

2009. Flowers instead of Bugattis. Four Bugattis and one Siata stood behind these arches 26 years ago. (Courtesy Kevin Herron)

described as a stubborn eccentric, and a person who was not only neglecting his cars, but also his historic farm. The accommodation was damp, and the cleanliness of his house left a lot to be desired; and to cap it all, his identity was divulged, albeit indirectly. Although his name was not printed, the article revealed that the owner was born in Geneva; was 54 years old; lived on a 19th century farm in a hamlet about 100 kilometres south of Paris, and was a well-known French wine journalist. Because Dovaz had more than earned his spurs in the field of French viticulture, and was already an expert on that subject in France and beyond, it was not difficult to determine the identity of the owner of the collection.

As the information in the article was clearly provided by someone who had been there, Hesselmann is at pains to maintain – to this very day – that he has always kept his promise of confidentiality. However, Walther Wuttke, who met Dovaz in Paris, and later visited him at Villemaréchal, must have obtained the name and address from someone ... even though it may have been a professional exchange of information. Wuttke,

2009. This place was populated by Aston Martins, Ferraris, Lancias, Hotchkisses, etc. during the early 1980s. The new Peugeot is far from an acceptable substitute. (Courtesy Kevin Herron)

incidentally, had also promised not to reveal the location and the name.

Exodus of classic cars

The damage, however, had already been done, and Dovaz was visited by all types of people, including many aspiring purchasers who thought they would be able to acquire a classic car for 'next to nothing.'

Some even demanded that Dovaz respond to them in English. When he stated that under no circumstances would he sell any of his collection, he was abused and reproached about the terrible condition of his vehicles. Thieves and souvenir hunters climbed over the walls, and even helicopters buzzed around the farm. The absolute low point came when a thief used an oxyacetylene cutter to remove the entire front axle of a Bugatti Atalante. Dovaz was given no peace and the situation became completely untenable. As he did not want to dispose of his cars, he took the only decision that he reasonably could; he decided to move the collection.

In 1984, the entire collection was moved to a secret location. Again, it was Guido Bartelomeo, who informed Hesselmann that there would be a removal of all the cars, which meant that Hesselmann was able to photograph the exodus of the cars. The whole project was organised and paid for by Michel Dovaz. He was furious – furious at Hesselmann, the journalists, the thieves, and the prying eyes.

Two years later, in 1986, Hesselmann, together with the author Halwart Schrader, published his famous book about the collection, entitled *Sleeping Beauties*. Bearing in mind the events of the past, and owing to the cooperation by the author, the tone of the book was somewhat more reticent than the *Stern* article. The address and identity of Michel Dovaz were not revealed (he was called 'Pierre' in the book), and his character was presented in a better light. Hesselmann was well aware of what had happened in the past, and what his role had been, but this did not discourage him from publishing the book. Indeed, *Sleeping Beauties* was a resounding success.

In October 2007, more than twenty years after the first edition, a new book[2] about the collection, by Hesselmann and Schrader, appeared. It was an expanded edition, including the information from 1983 and 1984. Although the authors were well informed about the developments surrounding the collection, no mention of them was made in the new book. Hesselmann and Schrader were quite happy to give the impression that the 'fairy tale' (as they called it) continued unabated.

But, perhaps, after 25 years, this is the right time to redress the balance, and hear the other side of the story.

Opposite: the relocation of the Dovaz collection, 1984. (Courtesy Didier Lainé/Editions LVA)

The collector who is not a collector at all

CRSO

Just imagine, you're twenty years old, you're passionate about cars and mechanical engineering, and you like nothing better than speeding around the Paris region in fast sports cars. Yes, indeed, in 1948, Michel Dovaz was having the time of his life!

During that period, the lack of traffic meant he was able to indulge his interest to the full; and, more importantly, unique cars from the 1930s were going for a song. An exceptional Bugatti, a unique Cord, a stately twelve-cylinder Lincoln Continental, or a thoroughbred Alfa Romeo, were all within the reach of a young man such as Michel Dovaz, who was fascinated by technology and speed. In the years immediately after the war, many of these splendid cars were kept roadworthy because there was no other means of transport. When industry and the economy picked up again, such cars were normally scrapped, and replaced by smarter, more comfortable, and cheaper mass-production models. There was no longer a demand for older, extravagant cars, however fast they were. Nobody had the faintest idea that, about thirty years later, these sports cars would be worth a fortune, not even Michel. He bought them cheaply, and drove them around until they developed mechanical or other problems. He then parked them near his flat, in the streets of Montmartre in Paris, bought another car, and so the cycle repeated itself. Dovaz, however, had one unusual characteristic – he was unable to part with his vehicles, and as nobody wanted them at the time, there was no reason to do so. He did try to sell one car by advertising it, but received no replies whatsoever. All Michel wanted to do was to drive his cars, and when he couldn't sell them, he simply kept them as souvenirs.

In 1958, the young Dovaz had about twenty cars parked in the streets of Montmartre, including nine Bugattis. The Paris police insisted that during the hours of darkness, the cars should be equipped with a red light for safety reasons. To prevent the lights being stolen, Dovaz used petroleum lanterns, that he placed in the locked cars. This resulted in a series of blackened canopies.

The complaints from local residents posed another problem. Michel therefore hired a hanger at Montlhéry race course, where he was able to park the cars, with the added advantage that the circuit was permanently patrolled by the army.

Somewhere in the back of his mind, Michel Dovaz had the intention of displaying the vehicles in a museum, but the social situation at the time was not propitious. Everyone was occupied with postwar reconstruction, and there was absolutely no interest in a museum of specialist cars dating from before, or shortly after, World War II. The collection continued to grow, however, and in 1964 Michel was forced to relocate his stable of cars, now comprising more than forty vehicles, for the second time.

Michel Dovaz's membership card of the French race drivers association AGACI, from 1958.
(Courtesy Pierre-Yves Laugier)

Almost twenty years of peace

❦

As it was, Michel Dovaz's career did not develop around automobiles, but was centred in the field of viticulture. At the start of the sixties, he was contributing to leading wine journals in France and other countries; was a member of many prominent juries, and had written various authoritative books about wine.

In 1964, when he was a widely respected wine expert and journalist, he purchased a 19th century farm in the middle of the hamlet of Villemaréchal, opposite the church. The farm was replete with stables and sheds, which meant he could store most of the cars under cover. Dust, bird droppings and moss may well have gathered on the cars, but rust had hardly any chance of forming. Michel lived there surrounded by his collection, each car holding a memory for him, as he had driven every one of them. Nobody in the village was aware, that behind the walls of this farm stood such a wonderful collection. Every Frenchman with land of any size had one or two discarded cars on his property, so it seemed that there was nothing to get excited about. Naturally enough, the villagers had often seen unusual cars passing through the entrance to Dovaz's farm, but in these country areas a person's privacy was well-guarded. So the collection grew steadily to nearly sixty cars, which was the situation at the time of the photo session.

Dovaz hosted regular gatherings of car enthusiasts at his farm where, over a glass of excellent wine, the guests discussed cars and various other subjects, such as literature, wine and politics. He would become very upset if a guest made a condescending remark about his cars. The offending person was personally escorted off the property, and was never invited back again.

Dovaz did not consider his cars to be a collection. Even today he says of himself, "I am not a collector." For him, all cars are manifestations of technology, which he admires; the mechanical part of the car being more important for him than the bodywork. He has no intention of restoring the cars to perfect condition, although he has often thought about doing them up. The cars (the last of which arrived in the middle of the '70s) form part of his life. His argument is that real beauty does not perish beneath thick dust; and in addition, he has been so busy with his career, that when a certain point was reached where he had so many cars, it would have been impossible to restore them all.

Then, Guido Bartolomeo turned up with the photographer, who was able to gain the confidence of Michel, and get down to work with his team. This was the beginning of the end for the 'sleeping beauties' at Villemaréchal.

VILLEMARÉCHAL

In the village people didn't know much about the hidden collection. (Hottendorff/op de Weegh)

The former Dovaz property in Villemaréchal, France, 2007. (Hottendorff/op de Weegh)

The secret castle

CR&O

After the many articles in the international automobile press, and especially the damning review of September 1983, in the German magazine *Stern,* Michel Dovaz's life was turned completely upside down.

As well as being harassed by prying eyes, fortune hunters, the Press and thieves, Michel was torn by doubt. There was a large group of people who condemned him for the picture painted by the *Stern* article. The path of least resistance would have been to sell the cars, and then carry on leading a peaceful life. But, two things held Dovaz back. The first, was his resolute character, which urged him not to 'throw in the towel' straightaway; and the second – however strange it might sound – was his strong attachment to the cars. Under no circumstances did he want to get rid of them. Finally, Michel decided to move the whole collection to Château de Folmont in Bagat-en-

One of the relocation trucks in Villemaréchal, 1984. (Courtesy Didier Lainé/Editions LVA)

Quercy, the property of a wine journalist friend. Here, he could carry on his life in peace, with his beloved cars.

The move took place in the spring of 1984, and to let the world know that there was nothing left in Villemaréchal, he allowed Herbert Hesselmann to make another photo-reportage for the international press. The transport company that moved nearly sixty cars on eight transporters, from Villemaréchal to Bagat-en-Quercy – a distance of more than 650 kilometres – demanded a substantial sum for this unusual transport task. The press and various inquisitive people followed the transports like vultures, almost to Bagat-en-Quercy. The last fifty kilometres were covered in darkness, when the transports felt certain that they weren't being followed, but on the very first evening that the cars arrived, Michel was robbed once again.

Château de Folmont is located on a hill. At the rear, about three minutes' walk downhill, there is an old, very roomy German bunker from the Second World War. Here, Michel Dovaz stored his most valuable cars. The others vehicles were parked around the bunker on open ground. As the climate there was predominantly dry this was not a problem for the forty- to fifty-year-old cars. And once again, Michel Dovaz was at peace with his memories.

Where the collection was relocated in 1984: Château de Folmont, near Bagat-en-Quercy, France, 2007. Some of the cars were stored in the small barn in the bottom photo. (Hottendorff/op de Weegh)

The museum in Sarlat,
and the tax authorities

❧❧

At that time a young Frenchman, Thierry Giovannoni, was fully involved in classic cars and rallies. He had learned about the existence of the collection, via the various publications. He was especially interested in the Alfa Romeo 6C 2500 Competizione, of which, only three had been made in around 1949, and one of which had been lost, due to a fatal accident in the early fifties. In 1987, Giovannoni wanted, whatever the cost, to enter this exclusive car in a rally in Morocco.

Meanwhile, at the insistence of Guido Bartolomeo (who had remained friends with Dovaz until his death in 2005, despite what had happened), Michel Dovaz had allowed the Competizione to be restored in Narbonne, whereupon, in 1984, the two drove the historic car in the Mille Miglia. Bartolomeo was an Alfa enthusiast, and completely 'mad' about the Competizione. He had tried for years to buy the sports car from Michel, but had not succeeded, although the car was kept in a shed at Bartolomeo's place until 1988.

Thierry Giovannoni had never met Michel Dovaz, but was invited to the Château de Folmont for dinner, where he made the acquaintance of Michel, and the special collection of cars. At that time Giovannoni was busy with the organisation of the 1988 motor show in Bordeaux, and hit upon the idea of using two of the cars from the Dovaz collection, with the theme: 'Auto Chic, Auto Choc.' He suggested it to Dovaz, who replied laconically: "Why not? It's a quirky idea." They agreed that Giovannoni should use two

Bugattis from the collection, ie the Type 55 Faux Cabriolet, and the Type 57 Fontana. The cars were collected in secret. At Bordeaux, Giovannoni created a stand with a 'natural environment,' and displayed the two cars in their unrestored state, between the gleaming new vehicles. To Giovannoni's and Dovaz's satisfaction, the event was a great success.

Encouraged by this, Giovannoni conceived the idea of a museum. He knew of an empty garage in Sarlat that would be excellent for this purpose. He discussed his plan with Dovaz, and was able to persuade him to make available twenty five special, unrestored cars, as well as the restored Alfa Romeo 6C 2500 Competizione. The realisation and management of the museum was placed in the hands of José Ramos, director of the garage, and he displayed the cars in a special and perceptive way, in situations drawn from real life. The museum opened in 1989, and was a great success. Ramos and Giovannoni received a great deal of recognition, and many compliments, but once again negative voices were heard in the press. There was talk of the 'disgraceful state of the cars,' and the 'loss of French cultural heritage,' which wounded Dovaz deeply.

In the meantime, something else had happened. In 1987, at Christie's auction house in London, a Bugatti Type 41 Royale was auctioned for the astronomical sum of 5.5 million pounds sterling. This caused a furore, not only in the classic car world, but also elsewhere. Classic cars were compared to Picasso's and Rembrandts. The price of classic cars rose at

The Bugatti Type 55 Faux Cabriolet, being unloaded near the museum in Sarlat, 1989.
(Courtesy current owner)

breathtaking speed, and this attracted the attention of many interested parties.

One of these was the tax authorities, and Michel Dovaz did not escape their attention. Due to the articles about the collection, and the setting up of the museum at Sarlat, the French tax authorities had got wind of the fact that Dovaz owned a priceless collection of cars. The value of the cars was considerable, which threatened to result in an enormous tax bill. However, in 1989 there was a change in the status of classic cars, and most prices plummeted, so the tax authorities had no real case against him. In 1990, due to the possible tax assessment, as well as the continuing storm of criticism, Michel Dovaz decided to close the museum and disperse the collection. After forty years in existence, the collection was finally administered the 'coup de grace.'

Thierry Giovannoni helped Dovaz sell most of the cars – about forty altogether. These included the nine Bugattis, which Dovaz disposed of because, of all his cars, these had the highest value and he expected the tax assessment of these models to be severe. Seven of the nine Bugattis were sold for 1.2 million pounds sterling, (a stronger currency than the French franc) to Jean-Michel Bonabosch, a pharmaceutical industrialist from Lyon. He very quickly resold three of the cars, and owing to financial problems in 1993, was forced to sell the other four Bugattis at auction. The auction took place on 16 March, in 1993, in the Hôtel des Ventes in Lyon-Brotteaux; the auctioneer being Jean-Claude Anaf.

MUSÉE AUTOMOBILE DE SARLAT

R.G.O Présente

FANTASMES AUTOMOBILES

Musèe Automobile de SARLAT
Rue Louis Mie Sarlat 24200

OUVERT TOUS LES
JOURS SAUF
LUNDI MATIN
RUE LOUIS-MIE - SARLAT
53 31 17 14

R.G.O.
PRÉSENTE
UN MUSÉE AUTOMOBILE
PRODUIT ET RÉALISÉ PAR
José RAMOS
SUR UNE IDÉE ORIGINALE DE
Thierry GIOVANNONI
« *Fantasmes automobiles* »

ACTE 1, SCÈNE 1 :

En 1929, Errett Loban Cord crée le type L 29, 1re traction avant américaine de série sur les données d'Harry Miller. Le modèle présenté est une limousine six glaces de 1929.

En 1934 la CORD 810/812 fait son apparition. Toujours à traction avant, elle est équipée d'un V8. Le modèle présenté est une Berline WESTCHESTER. Elle dispose d'un compresseur centrifuge SCHWITZER-CUMMINS, développe près de 200 CV, et atteint les 100 km/h en moins de 14 secondes.

La scène présentée est une reconstitution d'un plateau de tournage, avec au volant de la Cord 812 JAMES DEAN. Grand amateur de Cord et pilote de course, il trouva la mort au volant d'une Barquette Porsche RS.

ACTE 1, SCÈNE 2 :

La Firme Anglaise JOWETT proposait avant la guerre de robustes berlines aux lignes aérodynamiques équipées d'un 1 500 cm³ 4 cylindres à plat. En 1949, Eberan von Eberhorst poussa le petit 1 500 à 60 cv et l'installa dans un châssis tubulaire de sa fabrication. La firme reprit ce modèle à son compte, la JUPITER était née et bien née puisqu'elle remporta la classe 1 500 aux 24 heures du Mans en 1950/51/52. Le modèle présenté sorti directement d'une B.D., fut carrossé par GHIA.

Pages 26-28: Advertising flyer of the museum Phantasmes Automobiles in Sarlat, France, 1989-90.
(Courtesy Thierry Giovannoni)

ACTE 1, SCÈNE 3 :

Ce petit coin de garage des années 50 est sans conteste le royaume du passionné : outre les 2 «monstres sacrés»; ALFA ROMÉO CABRIOLET 2,5 litres 1948 et ASTON MARTIN DB 2/4, une multitude de pièces détachées et accessoires aujourd'hui rarissimes (Bugatti, Lotus, Alfa, Aston...) comblera les connaisseurs. L'ASTON DB 2/4 présentée, a participé 2 fois aux 24 heures du Mans aux mains de E. Da Silva Ramos.

ACTE 1, SCÈNE 6 :

Une scène grand luxe, où se côtoient, Grand Bis de Course de 1884, une magnifique collection de bouchons de radiateurs et certainement l'une des plus belles réalisations de Jean Bugatti : le faux cabriolet « TYPE 55 ». Sorti à 40 exemplaires seulement, le « TYPE 55 » possède un 8 cyl. en ligne à 2 A.C.T. et compresseur, développe 135 cv, possède une vitesse de pointe de 180 km/h et les 100 km/h sont atteints en 13 secondes.

ACTE 1, SCÈNE 7 :

Une ALFA ROMÉO 2,3 litres, 6 cylindres, double arbre à cames en tête, dans une scène «Mille Miglia», quoi de plus naturel ?
Cette berlinette carrossée par Touring en 1937 disposait déjà de 4 roues indépendantes, d'une carrosserie en aluminium et de 135 cv.

ACTE 1, SCÈNE 8 :

Un terrain vague, une vieille voiture finissant ses jours sous les coups de marteaux et les cailloux de 4 enfants de la rue. Voici une scène classique d'une certaine époque.
La vieille dame est cependant bien née puisqu'il s'agit d'une Bugatti «TYPE 49» 8 cyl. I A.C.T., 3 soupapes par cylindre et double allumage. 475 «TYPE 49» seront construites entre 1930 et 1934.

ACTE 1, SCÈNE 9 :

La sculpture est un art majeur chez Bugatti puisque de Luigi, grand-père d'Ettore Bugatti à Rembrandt son frère en passant par Carlo son père, 3générations ont sculpté.
Il était donc naturel de trouver ici une BUGATTI 57 SC ATALANTE naissant de la pierre sous le marteau adroit d'un sculpteur de génie.

ACTE 1, SCÈNE 10 :

La LANCIA DILAMBDA 8 cyl. en V était à l'époque la voiture des archevêques, le poids excessif de cette limousine d'apparat (2 800 kg) avait forcé ses ingénieurs créateurs a intégrer au châssis 2 crics hydrauliques afin de lever le véhicule en cas de panne.

——————————— 1er étage

ACTE 2, SCÈNE 1 :

Un écrin de rêve pour une voiture de rêve. Il y eut 3 Ferrari 340 AMERICA carrossées par GHIA. Celle-ci fut la propriété de Marcel-Paul Cavalier directeur de la Société Pont-à-Mousson avant d'être celle du prince Rainier de Monaco, Les 4,1 litres du Moteur Lampredi propulsaient ce coupé a plus de 250 km/h dans une ambiance plus «racing» que «grand tourisme».

ACTE 2, SCÈNE 2 :

« Il est possible de tout perdre dans la vie sauf sa dignité... » semble se dire ce vieil homme, après avoir transformé son véhicule en résidence secondaire pour clochard. Surtout quand cette résidence s'appelle... Rolls Royce Silver Cloud III.

ACTE 2, SCÈNE 3 :

8 cylindres, 4 840 cm³, 2 arbres à cames en tête, 2 carburateurs Schebler, et compresseur 200 cv à 4 000 tours/minutes, 65 véhicules fabriqués, telles sont les caractéristiques de ces 2 BUGATTI «TYPE 50», l'une carrossée par Vizcaya l'autre par Jean Bugatti, 2 autres BUGATTI 57 (Ventoux et Berline sans montants Gangloff) terminent ce stand à la gloire du constructeur de Molsheim.

ACTE 1, SCÈNE 4 :

Quel amateur d'automobiles anciennes n'a pas rêvé de trouver au fond d'une grange, un modèle exceptionnel ?
Ce fantasme prend corps, dans cette scène, sous les traits d'un coupé BUGATTI 44 carrossé en «FIACRE», et d'une BUGATTI 57 Carrosserie «FONTANA».

ACTE 1, SCÈNE 5 :

La TATRA est sans doute le projet le plus célèbre né sur la planche à dessin de Hans Ledwinka.
Son « arête dorsale » caractéristique lui confère un petit air « préhistorique » et s'intègre parfaitement dans ce terrarium peuplé d'iguanes et de varans vivants.

ACTE 2, SCÈNE 4 :

LANCIA AURELIA B 20 PININFARINA 6 cylindres 2,5 litres, pour un pique-nique de classe : une scène typique des années 50.

ACTE 2, SCÈNE 5 :

« La Brocante de chez Lulu ». Une petite guinguette, une brocante originale autour d'une LINCOLN CONTINENTAL V 12 et d'une PANHARD DYNAMIC 6 cyl. sans soupapes, il ne manque que la Marne et un petit air d'accordéon !

ACTE 2, SCÈNE 6 :

ASTON MARTIN DB 2/4 « RACING », LOTUS ELITE en pleine bagarre ; cela pourrait être au Nürburgring ou à la Targa Florio, ou bien tout simplement une course de V.E.C. (véhicule d'époque de compétition).

ACTE 2, SCÈNE 7 :

Elle est certainement la seule survivante, elle a été pilotée par Jean-Manuel Fangio, elle s'est illustrée aux Mille Miglia et a la Targa Florio, elle est d'une beauté rarissime, c'est la célèbre ALFA ROMÉO 2,5 litres « COMPETIZIONE ».

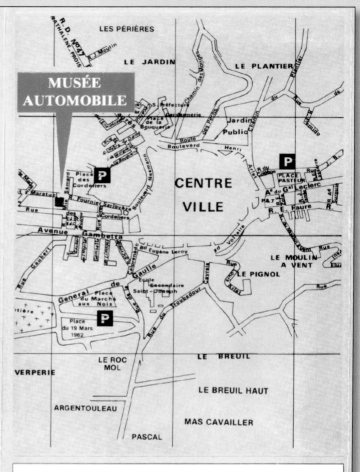

OUVERTURE

LUNDI : 14 H 30 À 20 H
MARDI - MERCREDI - JEUDI 10 H - 20 H
VENDREDI - SAMEDI - DIMANCHE 10 H - 22 H

PRIX D'ENTRÉE : **25 F**
GROUPE : **15 F**
GRATUIT JUSQU'À 12 ANS

RENSEIGNEMENTS :

MUSÉE AUTOMOBILE DE SARLAT
RUE LOUIS-MIE - 24200 SARLAT
TÉL. 53 31 17 14

Ferrari 340 in a temple diorama in Sarlat, 1989-90. (Courtesy Editions LVA)

Cord 812 and Panhard Dynamic at Château de Sanxet, 2007. (Hottendorff/op de Weegh)

Rolls-Royce Silver Cloud III in Sarlat, decorated as the home of a hobo, 1989-90. (Courtesy Didier Lainé)

Bugatti quartet in Sarlat, 2 Type 50s and 2 Type 57s, 1989-90. (Courtesy Didier Lainé)

Both Cords and the red Lotus on arrival at Château de Sanxet, 1990.
(Courtesy Bertrand de Passemar)

From his original collection, Michel Dovaz retained nineteen cars; four of which went to his private castle in the Périgord, with the remaining fifteen being transferred to the Château de Sanxet in Pomport, the property of his good friend Bertrand de Passemar. Of these fifteen cars, five have been sold and two transferred to De Passemar, himself the owner of a collection of old cars. De Passemar, who speaks with fervour and respect about his friend, Michel Dovaz, runs a large wine business, and maintains the car museum as a hobby. Today, the cars can be viewed for a small entrance fee.

The ten cars of the Dovaz Collection – eight of which are still the property of Dovaz – are displayed in an unrestored state, between the twenty five restored cars of the De Passemar collection. However, they are all in a better condition than is suggested in the Hesselmann photos of nearly a quarter of a century ago, even though they have not been touched since 1983 – except for a spot of cleaning.

Later on, in the nineties, a brilliant young lawyer won a case brought by Dovaz against the French tax authorities. For the collection and the Bugattis, however, it was too late ...

Bugatti Type 57 Fontana (#57407) during the auction in Lyon, 1993.
(Courtesy Jaap Braam Ruben Collection)

Bugatti Type 57 Ventoux (#57286) during the auction in Lyon, 1993. (Courtesy Jaap Braam Ruben Collection)

Michel Dovaz in 2007

꧁꧂

On 3 November 2007, we were able to speak to Michel Dovaz (who was then 79 years old) about his collection of cars. When we visited him on that memorable Saturday, at his flat in Paris, we were the first to have interviewed him since 1983.

After everything we had read and heard about the man, we were indeed somewhat nervous, and had formed a rather negative picture of him. This was completely belied by what we found. We met a totally different person to the one described by Hesselmann and Schrader, and without doubt, completely different to the one portrayed in the *Stern* article of 1983. We were welcomed with champagne by a hospitable, intelligent, friendly and self-confident man, who was still leading a very active life. The first thing that Dovaz asked us was what type of vehicle we had arrived in. Ard replied: "A Volvo C70 T5." To which Dovaz retorted, "That's an old man's car." The atmosphere was very relaxed, and we felt perfectly at ease. Michel Dovaz related his absorbing story in an animated fashion, and answered our questions unreservedly. Now and again, he gave the impression of being a mischievous child. As he spoke, he gestured frequently and sometimes winked impishly. It was striking, that during that demanding interview, – which lasted almost three and a half hours – he was able to recall almost every detail of the past, and peppered his replies with many vivid anecdotes. Michel had a really good sense of humour, and was able to captivate and amuse us throughout the conversation. He agreed to help us with the book

Left to right: Kay Hottendorff, Ard op de Weegh and Arnoud op de Weegh visiting Michel Dovaz on 3 November 2007. (Hottendorff/op de Weegh)

in any way he could, and when we departed – after having promised to remain in contact – all three of us were very pleased to have met this remarkable man.

Michel Dovaz did not resemble 'Pierre' in the two books by Hesselmann and Schrader, and he was completely unlike the 'Pierre', described by Wuttke. We met a humorous man in a tidy Paris apartment, who was enthusiastic and revealing in his emotions, with a feeling for values and his fellow man. Without a doubt, for someone of his age, he is a man of the times.

The most striking thing was that he claimed never to have seen Hesselmann's book, and also that he did not want to either: "I have never seen the book by Mr Hesselmann, therefore, I have no idea what it contains," he said. Indeed, throughout our visit – and we had both books with us – he showed hardly any interest in them at all.

Epilogue

❦

It is clear that Michel Dovaz was instrumental in saving various special cars, including nine Bugattis, which surely would have otherwise gone to the breakers, as at that time their only value was the scrap value of the material from which they were made. In retrospect, the classic car world, and the Bugatti world in particular, should be very grateful to Michel. In their restored state, the cars now provide a great deal of pleasure to many people.

Directly and indirectly, Michel Dovaz suffered a great injustice during the 1980s, owing to the publicity associated with his collection. His nature was too trusting. He should have established some of his rights in law, and invoked a penalty clause if his secret was revealed in any way. He tried to institute legal proceedings, but apart from the action against *Geo*, abandoned the attempts. However, it is easy to be wise after the event. It is striking that, even in the 2007 edition of the book about the collection, the photographer and his author still refer to the owner as 'Pierre' – though the entire classic car world has known that the collection belonged to Michel Dovaz for many years. Perhaps they are emphasizing that even after 25 years they are keeping faith with Dovaz.

In one aspect however, they have certainly not done so; Hesselmann promised never to publish any photos of Michel Dovaz, but the 2007 book contains various photos in which Dovaz is clearly identifiable.

The property in Villemaréchal as seen from the street in 2007. (Hottendorff/op de Weegh)

In May 2007, we visited the farm in Villemaréchal that had once belonged to Michel Dovaz. There was something disconsolate about it; something about the place that had been destroyed, and that could never be replaced. As we stood there, we were overcome by a sense of mystery; we even began speaking in whispers. It was as if the ghosts of Michel's cars were still around. Here, nearly a quarter of a century ago, the desire for wealth and fame triumphed over a man's attachment to a collection, and his cherished memories.

It is a pity, that such a distorted picture of Michel Dovaz prevailed for so many years. This remarkable Frenchman deserves better. His dream should not have been destroyed. It was taken from him, even though he had done nothing to deserve it.

2007. The gates of the former property of Michel Dovaz. (Hottendorff/op de Weegh)

The automobiles of
Michel Dovaz

Introduction

☙❧

It is difficult to determine exactly how many automobiles Michel Dovaz owned. Estimates vary between the 50 vehicles, mentioned in the book, *Sleeping Beauties*[1], and the 70 which Dovaz himself talked about.

On the basis of the photographs printed in the *Sleeping Beauties* books[1, 2] and two videos from around 1983, we made out exactly 55 different vehicles, and were able to identify all of these. However, it is very probable that a few more vehicles were added to the collection between 1984 and 1990. The only reason why these vehicles are not known, is probably because the photographs taken after 1984 are largely restricted to the 26 vehicles exhibited at the musée de Sarlat.

Chateau de Sanxet is today home to a Dovaz car, which did not become part of the collection until after 1984 – a 1962 Alfa Romeo. After 1984, Dovaz also became the owner of a DeSoto and a Maserati, and presumably several more cars, which we know nothing about. We can therefore, account for 58 of up to 70 vehicles.

What factors, however, did Michel Dovaz take into account when buying his vehicles? If we group the vehicles from Villemaréchal according to their countries of origin, all but two of the vehicles come from the great automotive nations of France (17 cars); Italy (16); Britain (11); and the USA (9). Germany was only represented by a single Volkswagen, dating from the 1970s. This was indeed a clear vote. Dovaz's preference for certain vehicle

models was equally clear. In 1983, nine Bugattis, nine Lancias, four Alfa Romeos and four Lincolns accounted for just under half of the collection at Villemaréchal.

Moreover, it is remarkable that Dovaz possessed two or more examples of many vehicle types, for example the Aston Martin DB2, the Lincoln Continental, the Lotus Elite and the Rolls-Royce Silver Cloud III. More particularly, the collection contained luxurious, very rare or even unique automobiles, as well as cars with a special race history.

Michel Dovaz never saw himself as a collector who hunted down missing pieces to incorporate into his collection. He bought cars to drive; to drive them fast and to enjoy them. If the vehicles were beyond repair, Dovaz bought another of the same type, or turned to the next model. He was actually a man who had much more in common with automobile manufacturers of the calibre of Ettore Bugatti, than a collector who collects cars like stamps, and preserves them in an album made of concrete and steel ... condemned all too often to immobility. Dovaz was also fascinated by the unusual; by special technology. Many of his cars featured technical innovations, and were ahead of their time. There was, for example, the front-wheel-drive of the 1929 Cord L-29, and the sleeve valve engine of the 1930s Panhard & Levassor Dynamic, although the latter never became popular. In this context, Dovaz was also attracted to mass-produced vehicles, as long as they were unusual or

Michel Dovaz. (Courtesy Michel Dovaz)

strange enough in some way: the Citroën 2CV, the Citroën H or the Panhard Dyna X.

In short, the individualist Michel Dovaz looked for, and found, cars which were different, and thus reflected his own personality and lifestyle.

The appendix includes a list of all 58 known 'sleeping beauties' and a site plan of the vehicle locations, as found at the property at Villemaréchal in 1983. The list contains references to the page numbers in the book *Sleeping Beauties*[2] published in 2007, to facilitate the correct attribution of the photographs from the 1980s.

The nine Bugattis presented in the Sleeping Beauties book

❧❧

No one really knows how a make of car becomes the stuff of legends. Suffice to say that strong leadership qualities, and exclusive products of the highest quality with the added dimension of breathtaking design, are certainly no impediment. The Bugatti make combined all these amazing qualities. The company's founder was Ettore Bugatti, the son of an artistic family from Milan, who was born in 1881. As a young man, Ettore worked as a designer for various car manufacturers, including de Dietrich, Mathis and Deutz. In 1909 Ettore decided to establish his own car manufacturing business in Molsheim, a small town in the Alsace region, which was then part of Germany. Over the next few decades, the spider's web of myths that surrounded Bugatti was woven, largely due to countless successes in motor racing. Bugatti was not partial to compromises; he built his cars exactly as he envisaged them. Modern keywords, such as 'customer-driven', were not part of his vocabulary. For instance, Ettore refused to allow the King of Albania to own a Type 41 Royale, simply because he was disgusted by the latter's table manners. The king had to journey home from Alsace in the same vehicle that had brought him there – the train.

In the 1930s, the ingenious designs of Ettore's son, Jean Bugatti, contributed to the growing success of the company. Among Jean's masterpieces were such rare models as the Type 50 and Type 55, and the successful Type 57. However, the downfall of the Bugatti company was sealed by several fateful events. In 1939, Jean was killed while performing test drives on a country road. During World War II, the factory in Molsheim was seized by the Germans and used for the production of arms. Later, Ettore was accused of being a collaborator, and was not cleared of the allegation until shortly before his death in 1947. Having lost the two geniuses who had been at the helm of the establishment, all attempts at recovery after the war were doomed to failure. In 1963, Hispano Suiza acquired what was left of the business.

The Bugatti make did not experience a reincarnation until the end of the 1980s, when it was initially restarted under Italian management. Since 1998, the company has been part of the Volkswagen conglomerate.

Of the 7800 Bugattis that were manufactured up to 1940, only about 2000 were preserved. All of them, without exception, are now highly coveted collectibles. In the 1950s, Bugattis, as well as most other pre-war cars were available at ridiculously low prices – scrap yard prices, so to speak. Bugattis that had sustained damage in accidents, or suffered engine failure were scrapped, while others were raided for parts. Some Bugattis even fought their final battles in local stock car races. Back then, very few people had the foresight to appreciate, and take good care of, these artefacts on wheels, but among these automotive enthusiasts were Fritz Schlumpf and Michel Dovaz. The two made their own, very special contributions to the preservation of these icons of automotive heritage and culture.

Jean Bugatti, left, (1909-1939) with his father Ettore (1881-1947). (Courtesy The Bugatti Trust)

During the 1960s, Swiss textile entrepreneur Fritz Schlumpf, and his brother, Hans, probably accumulated the world's most impressive automotive collection ever. The two were particularly fascinated with the vehicles made in nearby Molsheim: their collection of about 560 cars included precisely 151 Bugattis. Based on the fair market values of the cars back in that era, the Schlumpfs paid top money for everything Bugatti. The highly enthralling story of their passion and their museum, which is now owned by the French government, and located in Mulhouse, is described in detail in the book *Der Fall der Brüder Schlumpf* (*The Case of the Schlumpf Brothers*)[6].

Michel Dovaz caught the Bugatti fever early. He acquired his first Bugatti, a Type 49, in 1948. Over the years he owned 21 Bugattis, and he still had nine in the 1980s. Michel Dovaz knew the Schlumpfs personally, and eventually also became a target of their buying sprees, but he never gave in to them. Even back then he was smart enough, and stubborn enough to refuse offers that seemed too good to turn down. When his collection was sold in 1990, it was clear that sitting out the market had been the right approach financially. Dovaz sold seven Bugattis – all at once – for the amazing sum of about GBP 1.2 million. The remaining two were sold separately. The following pages are dedicated to descriptions of these nine Bugattis, which achieved worldwide acclaim in 1983 as the *Sleeping Beauties*.

1928 Bugatti Type 44 Fiacre
Chassis number 44580

The Type 44 was a popular touring car, of which about 1100 units were built from 1927 to 1930. Its eight-cylinder in-line engine developed 80hp from 3.0 litres of capacity. Michel Dovaz's Type 44 with chassis number 44580 has a somewhat traditional looking Fiacre body, reminiscent of the design of a stagecoach, which was a look that appealed greatly to Patron Ettore Bugatti.

The brand new vehicle was delivered to banker Baron Léo d'Erlanger in 1928. In 1946, René Veignant of Paris purchased the vehicle. Renowned French Bugatti specialist Henri Novo later equipped the car with Grebel headlights, and the aluminium wheels of a Bugatti Type 49. In the 1950s Michel Dovaz became the proud owner of the elderly car.

At Villemaréchal, the Type 44 was housed in an open barn, along with an Alfa Romeo 6C2500 Competizione and a Jowett Jupiter. By that time,

the roof cover had already rotted away and the wooden structure beneath was clearly visible. Later, at the Musée de Sarlat, the car was displayed next

Technical data:
Bugatti Type 44 Fiacre

Engine	.eight-cylinder in-line 2991cc
Bore x stroke.	.69 x 100mm
Compression ratio	.unknown
Power	.80hp
Top speed	.87mph
L x W x H	.unknown
Weight	.1100kg
Wheelbase	.312cm
Front track width.	.125cm
Rear track width..	.125cm
Production date	.1927-30 (T44)
Production number. ..	.1100 (T44)
Original price	.unknown

During the relocation to southern France, 1984. (Courtesy Didier Lainé/Editions LVA)

Bugatti #44580 with previous owner, Rene Veignant from Paris, 1940s/1950s.
(Courtesy current owner)

Decorated as 'barn find' at the museum in Sarlat, 1989-90.
(Courtesy Edmund Nankivell)

to a Bugatti Type 57 Fontana, in an authentic 'barn find' scene, covered with straw and surrounded by old agricultural implements. When the museum was closed in 1990, the Type 44 was sold to French pharmaceuticals manufacturer Jean-Michel Bonabosch, along with six other Bugattis. Just a year later, in 1991, Bonabosch sold the Type 44 and two other Bugattis to another Frenchman, who still owns the cars today.

The vehicle was completely restored between 1994 and 1997, and is now in a concourse condition. It was displayed not only at the Louis Vuitton Classics 1997, but also at the Paris Rétromobile trade show.

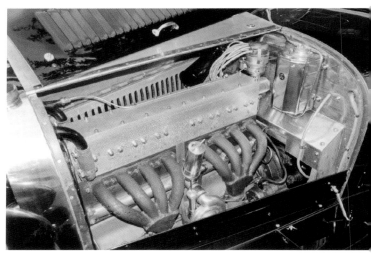

The completely restored car after 1997. (Courtesy current owner)

1931 Bugatti Type 49 Faux Cabriolet

Chassis number 49410

The T49 was the successor to the Type 44. In the period from 1930 to 1934, the company manufactured 470 of these cars. It had an eight-cylinder in-line engine, borrowed from the Type 44, which had been re-bored to just under 3.3 litres of capacity and now developed 85hp. A contemporary test report lauded the Type 49 as a successful blend of a comfortable carriage and lively sports car.

Michel Dovaz's Bugatti Type 49 was a so-called Faux Cabriolet by Gangloff. Such 'fake cabriolets' were quite fashionable back then. Fabric covered what was actually a hard top and imitation frame joints were installed to make the car look like a real cabriolet. This T49 was delivered to its original owner – Pierre Colin of Soisson, France – in April 1932.

Technical data:
Bugatti Type 49 Faux Cabriolet

Engine	eight-cylinder in-line 3257cc
Bore x stroke	72 x 100mm
Compression ratio	unknown
Power	85hp
Top speed	90mph
L x W x H	unknown
Weight	1100kg
Wheelbase	322cm
Front track width	125cm
Rear track width	125cm
Production date	1930-1934 (T49)
Production number	470 (T49)
Original price	FF 64,000 (#49410, 1932)

During the relocation to southern France, 1984. (Courtesy Didier Lainé/Editions LVA)

In Sarlat the Bugatti served as "... playground of the street urchins ..." (Courtesy Didier Lainé)

Bugatti #49410 with caravan and Paris plate, 1952. (Courtesy current owner)

Restored chassis, 1996. (Courtesy current owner)

*Bugatti #49410, completely restored, 1996.
(Courtesy current owner)*

The owner(s) who subsequently had possession of the car, until Michel Dovaz finally purchased it are unknown. Until 1983, the T49 was parked in a half-open barn at Villemaréchal. It was relatively well-shielded against the effects of wind and weather by two other Bugattis, that stood right in front of the arched access doors. At the Musée de Sarlat, the car was actually displayed in a diorama with street urchins, who were irreverently using it as an adventure toy.

This Bugatti was also sold in late 1990 to Jean-Michel Bonabosch, and was resold just a year later in 1991, together with the Type 44 and another Bugatti. The current French owner also had this vehicle restored to concourse condition.

1930 Bugatti Type 50 Million-Guiet
Chassis number 50113

The Type 46 was the little brother of the Type 41 Royale, and was nicknamed the 'Little Royale'. The two models were the most luxurious in the Bugatti range. In 1930, the Type 50 was launched as a sporty version of the Type 46.

Boasting a shorter chassis, a turbocharger and an optimized 5.0-litre eight-cylinder in-line engine, the Type 50 developed an impressive 225hp. Types 46 and 50 were launched during an economically unfavourable era. During the global economic crisis, luxury cars certainly did not sell well. The Type 46 generated about 400 orders and did quite a bit better than the Type 50, of which only 65 were made during the period from 1930 to 1934. Nonetheless, the Type 50 engine did provide a significant basis for Bugatti's future racing successes.

The Bugatti, bearing chassis number 50113 was one of the very first Type 50s to be built. The

Technical data:
Bugatti Type 50 Million-Guiet

Engine	eight-cylinder in-line 4972cc
Bore x stroke	86 x 107mm
Compression ratio	6.1:1
Power	225hp
Top speed	121mph
L x W	452 x 168cm
Weight	1173kg
Wheelbase	310cm
Front track width	138cm
Rear track width	138 cm
Production date	1930-34 (T50)
Production number	65 (T50)
Original price	FF 110,000 (#50113, 1930)

chassis was manufactured in October 1930, and delivered to Paris retailer Dominique Lamberjack in

The T50 on the right, together with Bugattis #57286 and #50131 being loaded after closure of the museum in Sarlat, 1990. (Courtesy previous owner of 50131/via Florian and Herbert Handlbauer)

January 1931. Paris-based body shop Million-Guiet was commissioned to finish the body. The shop was famous for its distinguished, edgy body styles, that did away with unnecessary embellishments. The body was made of aluminium panels based on a Vizcaya patent. It was self-supporting, and did not require the otherwise standard wooden frame. As a result, an unusually generous interior could be created. Large Bugatti Types 46 and 50, featuring the Million-Guiet body style are extremely rare. One other T50 is located in the United States and one T46 survived as part of the Schlumpf Collection in Mulhouse, France.

In 1936 the Bugatti 50113 made an appearance in the Jean Renoir movie *Le Crime de Monsieur Lange*[4]. After World War II, Mr Varenne from Paris, who owned the car at the time, made substantial conversions to it. When fitted with the mudguards of a late Bugatti Type 57, featuring integrated headlights, the car had completely different lines, which gave it a disharmonious look. Moreover, the straight windshield was replaced with a modern sloping version. All new parts were made from steel sheet instead of aluminium, and as a result, the Million-Guiet body style was basically no longer identifiable. Michel Dovaz purchased the car in this condition in July 1956. Although parked

The Bugatti T50 Million-Guiet in the 1930s before the remodelling. (Courtesy current owner)

During the restoration in New Zealand, 1993. (Courtesy current owner)

in a half-open barn at Villemaréchal, along with other Bugattis in 1983, the T50 seemed to be in amazingly good condition when it was moved in 1984, and displayed at the museum from 1989-90. At the end of 1990, this Bugatti was among those sold to Jean-Michel Bonabosch. As early as March 16 1993, it changed hands again during an auction at the Anaf Auction House in Lyon. However, the photographs taken during the auction reveal that the vehicle had suffered significant damage while it had been inappropriately stored by Michel Dovaz. At the auction, the unrestored car still fetched an impressive sum of FF 830,000. It was purchased by a German collector who still owns it today. He had the car restored completely in New Zealand, and all of the postwar modifications were reversed. After the emergence of new historical photographs, the car has undergone additional recent updates, so that it has now been restored to as close to its original condition as possible.

Opposite, top: In Molsheim after the first restoration, 1997. (Courtesy Jan Spiele)

Opposite, bottom: The completely restored T50, 2007. (Courtesy current owner)

Left and above: During the auction in Lyon, 1993. (Courtesy Jaap Braam Ruben Collection)

1931 Bugatti Type 50 Landaulet
Chassis number 50131

Ettore Bugatti had been hoping that his Type 50 would also be successful in long distance races, such as the Le Mans 24-Hour Race. For the race, slated to take place in Le Mans on June 13 and 14 1931, the company equipped a total of four Type 50s with open, four-seater Torpedo Sport bodies. One of these was a back-up model. The objective of the Le Mans man-made leather designs was to meet the race standards while reducing the weight of the car.

These cars could only be identified by their engine numbers, given that the factory cars were allocated chassis numbers only when they were resold after racing assignments.

The second Bugatti Type 50 in the Dovaz collection (Chassis 50131/Engine 22) is one of these factory cars; a fact that was also confirmed during a technical inspection performed in 2001 by expert Malcolm Gentry (GB), who discovered minor

differences in the frame when he compared it to series-manufactured frames.

Bugatti's three factory teams were considered

Technical data: Bugatti Type 50 Landaulet	
Engine	eight-cylinder in-line 4972cc
Bore x stroke	86 x 107mm
Compression ratio	6.1:1
Power	225hp
Top speed	121mph
L x W	452 x 168cm
Weight	1173kg
Wheelbase	310cm
Front track width	138cm
Rear track width	138cm
Production date	1930-34 (T50)
Production number	65 (T50)
Original price	unknown

The T50 during the relocation in Villemaréchal, 1984. (Courtesy Didier Lainé/Editions LVA)

Starting number 6 – Bugatti T50 with engine #22 – at the start of the race at Le Mans, 1931.
(Courtesy The Bugatti Trust)

After the accident, which happened during the same race, Le Mans, 1931. (Courtesy The Bugatti Trust)

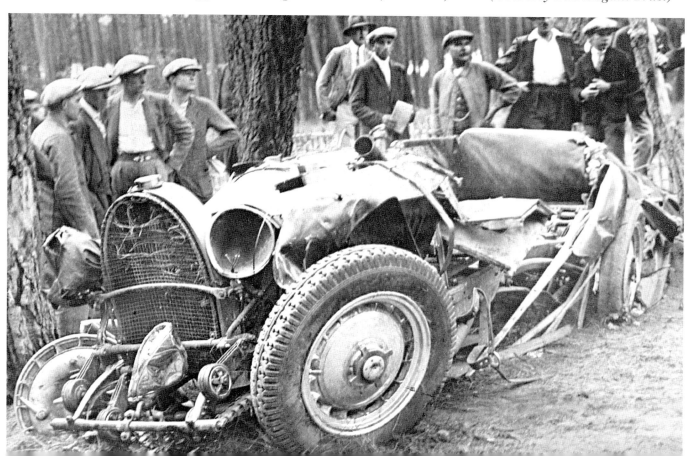

At the museum in Sarlat, 1989-90.
(Courtesy Editions LVA)

The engine of the T50 before restoration.
(Courtesy previous owner/via Florian and Herbert
Handlbauer)

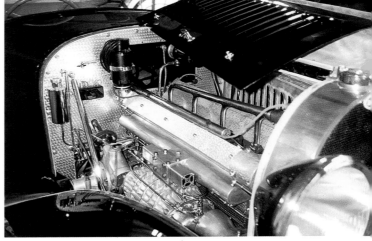

The almost completely restored T50 during the auction in Lyon, 1993.
(Courtesy Jaap Braam Ruben Collection)

odds-on favourites in the race. However, they ran into problems with the tyres from the start. The team that had been assigned start number 6 and race engine number 22 consisted of racing car driver Maurice Rost and Italian Earl Caberto Conelli. Maurice Rost was in the lead when the rear left tyre burst, causing a grave accident at a speed of 115mph. The car skidded off the track, killing a spectator, and ultimately crashing into a tree. Rost himself was lucky, as he was catapulted out of the vehicle during the accident. Nonetheless, he had to spend several months in a hospital. After the accident, Bugatti took both of the other factory teams (Albert Divo/Guy Bouriat and Achille Varzi/Louis Chiron) out of the race. The chassis of the vehicle that had been in the accident was not rebuilt. Engine number 22 was repaired and installed in one of the other factory cars, which had itself sustained engine damage at Le Mans. This vehicle was sold to Guy Bouriat, one of the drivers of the 1931 race, and was simultaneously assigned chassis number 50131. In 1933 it once again participated in the Le Mans race (Marie Desprez/ Pierre Bussienne, start number 3). In November 1933 it was sold to the director of a company called Le Blanc Minéral in Paris, Bougival. In 1934/35, he had a new body put on the Bugatti, possibly by Van Vooren in Courbevoie near Paris. Other sources make reference to an entry in the body book, indicating that, in August 1932, the Bugatti was fitted with a Jean Bugatti Landaulet body in cream and black at the Molsheim factory, and that it was sold to Sagnier, a dealer from Algiers, in March 1933.

Chassis and partly completed Le Mans body, 2007. (Courtesy Florian and Herbert Handlbauer)

During the auction in Lyon, 1993.
(Courtesy Jaap Braam Ruben Collection)

In completely restored condition, 2006.
(Courtesy Florian and Herbert Handlbauer)

Regardless of which of these versions of the story is accurate, the vehicle was acquired by Michel Dovaz in April, 1952. At Villemaréchal, the T50 was among those that enjoyed the privilege of being housed in the large and dry barn. In both photographic books[1,2] that cover the collection, this Bugatti was incorrectly identified as either a Type 40 or a Type 44. The Type 50 was among the vehicles displayed at the Musée de Sarlat from 1989-90.

This Type 50 was the only one of the Bugattis Jean-Michel Bonabosch acquired from Dovaz in late 1990 which he actually had restored. Along with three unrestored Bugattis, the vehicle was auctioned off by Anaf in Lyon in March, 1993. According to the auction catalogue, the only thing missing for it to be considered fully restored was the convertible top. The Frenchman, who still owns three other representatives of the Dovaz Bugattis today, was the winning bidder, and paid FF 1.7 million for the car. He commissioned completion of the restoration work, and had the paint job reversed to the original black-yellow combination. In 2001, however, he sold the vehicle to Herbert Handlbauer, an Austrian, who still owns it today. In 2007, the Bugatti Type 50 was fitted with a reconstruction of the 1931 Torpedo Sport Le Mans body in Italy. At the time, no decision had been made on the utilization of the still intact Landaulet body, which dates back to the 1930s.

During a Bugatti meeting in Austria, 2006. (Courtesy Fritz Berger/www.bestmoments.at)

1933 Bugatti Type 55 Faux Cabriolet
Chassis number 55233

Bugatti introduced its Type 55 in 1931. This sports car was equipped with a detuned version of the Type 51 racing engine. The eight-cylinder in-line engine developed 130hp from almost 2.3 litres of capacity. The company offered motoring enthusiasts a choice of two bodies, an open roadster design and a coupé in the style of a faux cabriolet.

Even today, the roadster, in particular, is considered one of Jean Bugatti's most magnificent designs. Unfortunately, only 38 Type 55s were made up to 1935. This makes the T55 one of the most coveted Bugatti types today. A car in mint condition would currently fetch a seven figure price in euros.

This Type 55 Faux Cabriolet with chassis number

Technical data:
Bugatti Type 55 Faux Cabriolet

Engine	.eight-cylinder in-line 2261cc
Bore x stroke	.60 x 100mm
Compression ratio	.6.6:1
Power	.130hp at 5000rpm
Top speed	.112mph
L x W x H	.420 x 155 x 130cm
Weight	.920kg
Wheelbase	.275cm
Front track width	.125cm
Rear track width	.125cm
Production date	.1931-35 (T55)
Production number ..	.38 (T55)
Original price	.unknown

Bugatti T55 Faux Cabriolet in Villemaréchal during the relocation, 1984. (Courtesy Didier Lainé)

With penny-farthing bicycle at the museum in Sarlat, 1989-90. (Courtesy Edmund Nankivell)

55233 was shipped to a dealer named Bucar in Zurich, Switzerland in 1933. It was acquired by Count Tositza who later sold the car to Michel Dovaz in October 1953. Thirty years later, it was housed in the now world-famous Bugatti/Cord barn at Villemaréchal. There the Type 55 was parked with the engine and wheels of a Type 35B fitted. Michel Dovaz had used these parts to make the car run after engine trouble made it unusable. The remainder of the T35B was probably destroyed as early as the 1950s. In both volumes of the photographic publications [1,2] that cover the collection, the T55 Coupé was sometimes referred to as a Type 44 or a Type 57.

This Bugatti was displayed at Sarlat as well, in a tableau including a lady with a penny-farthing

The still unrestored car, 1990. (Courtesy current owner)

bicycle, apparently suggesting that its history extended back to the pre-automotive era. The Type 55 was one of the seven sold to Jean Michel Bonabosch in 1990, who sold it just a year later to a Frenchman along with the previously described Type 44 and Type 49. All three are still in this owner's possession today; and he had the Type 55 updated to concourse condition between 1992 and 1997. In the process, the T35B engine was replaced by a correct T55 engine.

Top three photos: The Bugatti during the restoration, 1992-97. (Courtesy current owner)

The completely restored car, after 1997. (Courtesy current owner)

1937 Bugatti Type 57C Galibier
Chassis number 57476

The Galibier during the relocation to southern France, 1984.
(Courtesy Didier Lainé/Editions LVA)

Under Jean Bugatti's influence, as of 1934, the company modified its entire model policy, focusing on a single model. The Type 57, which was the successor of the Type 49, was offered ex-factory in a variety of standard body designs, chassis and engine options.

In addition to the 4-door Galibier saloon, the range included the two 2-door Coach Ventoux and Coupé Atalante versions, as well as two cabriolets, the Stelvio and the Aravis. The range was supplemented by niche models such as the 'Tank' racing car, which was victorious in Le Mans in 1937 and 1939, and also included the beautiful Atlantic. Only three of the latter breathtaking beauties were ever made. Given the vast range of factory-made bodies, fewer individual fabrications of bodies were made by other body coachbuilders. By 1940, 769 Type 57s had been produced, far too few considering that the company was pursuing a single model policy. Actually, it was a government contract for the assembly of rail cars that kept Ettore Bugatti afloat at the time. The power of the eight-cylinder in-line engine of almost 3.3 litres capacity varied from 135hp in the standard

At the museum in Sarlat, 1989-90. Note the body design without any B-pillar.
(Courtesy Dominique Delcros Archive)

Technical data:	
Bugatti Type 57C Galibier	
Engine	eight-cylinder in-line 3257cc
Bore x stroke..	72 x 100mm
Compression ratio..	6.6:1
Power	160hp
Top speed	109mph
L x W x H	460 x 175 x 150cm
Weight..	1500kg
Wheelbase..	330cm
Front track width..	135cm
Rear track width..	135cm
Production date	1934-40 (T57)
Production number. ..	769 (T57)
Original price	FF 82,000 (including body)

Type 57, to more than 160hp in the Type 57C (with supercharger), and to approximately 200hp in the Type 57SC model (with supercharger and shortened, deeper sports chassis).

From 1983 to 1990 Michel Dovaz owned a total of four Bugatti Type 57s, which are described in the following pages. The Galibier model was named after an Alpine pass, just like the Ventoux and Stelvio models.

Michel Dovaz's Type 57C Galibier, with chassis number 57476, was delivered new to Conchon Quinette in March 1937. The exact date Dovaz actually acquired the vehicle is not known. Nevertheless, he has stated that he remembers purchasing the car in the Paris suburb of Courbevoie from a man named Boyer.

Michel Dovaz replaced the original engine (#4C) with a substitute (#549), which had originally been in the Bugatti 57752. For the Galibier, this was definitely not a good choice, the supercharged #4C

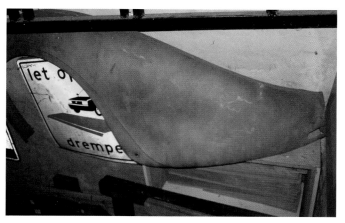

The preserved parts of the scrapped Galibier body, Belgium, 2008. (Hottendorff/op de Weegh)

engine developed 160hp and the standard engine developed 'only' 135hp.

At Villemaréchal, the car was housed in a half-open barn, along with the previously described T49 and T50 Million-Guiet. At the time, the body of the Galibier appeared to be in rather bad shape, probably because the front end of the vehicle had been exposed to the effects of the weather without any protection, given that it faced one of the open door arches.

When the Musée de Sarlat closed, the Galibier was the only Bugatti that was left behind unsold. The vehicle found a temporary home at the Château de Sanxet with Bertrand de Passemar. Ultimately, Michel Dovaz presented the car to Thierry Giovannoni, who had been one of the organizers of the Musée de Sarlat, as a token of gratitude for his services. The Galbier was later sold to Jean-Paul Gauban. Among the other subsequent owners were Colombier and Peter Schmitz from Eupen, Belgium. The latter had the body scrapped in 2000, although it had been in rather good condition according to Michel Dovaz, contrary to the initial assessment. Belgian Bugattist Jean Prick was able to save only the bonnet, front bumpers and doors.

A short time thereafter, the chassis was sold to another Belgian, Paul Engelen, who commissioned Briton, Rod Jolley to produce a replica body in Tourist Trophy Torpedo design. Allegedly, Engelen participated in the Mille Miglia with the car in 2004, although eligibility for participation in this elite event is subject to very strict standards pertaining to the original condition of the vehicles. In 2005, Engelen sold the car to an Austrian, who still owns it today.

When we showed Michel Dovaz photos depicting the current state of the Galibier, his response was less than enthusiastic. We quote: "Le simulacre qu'on en a fait est particulièrement stupide." ("The reproduction they've produced looks particularly stupid.")

Equipped with a Tourist Trophy replica body, Molsheim, 2003. (Courtesy Bernard Graf-Saner)

1935 Bugatti Type 57 Ventoux
Chassis number 57286

Bugatti Type 57 with chassis number 57286 was completed in February 1935 as a two-door Coupé Ventoux and shipped to Poisson in Morigny, Normandy, in October 1935. Francis Leclercq from Roubaix imported the vehicle into Belgium in 1947. Three years later he sold the car to Michel Dovaz, who re-imported it to France.

This vehicle is the one most closely associated with the Dovaz collection, probably because it had been unintentionally placed in a particularly photogenic setting inside the Villemaréchal barn, along with five other 1930s Bugatti, Cord and Alfa Romeo classics. Like no other, this car embodies the dream that haunts classic car enthusiasts, that of making their very own 'barn find' some day. Last, but not least, the Ventoux also made a bold statement on the covers of both volumes [1,2] of the photographic publications covering the collection and was also available in XXXL poster format (175cm x 112cm) at one point.

This car was also sold to Jean-Michel Bonabosch and presented for bidding at a 1993 auction in Lyon. Renowned Bugatti restoration expert André Lecoq placed the winning bid on the unrestored Type 57 and acquired it for FF 570,000. The original engine

Technical data:
Bugatti Type 57 Ventoux

Engine	eight-cylinder in-line 3257cc
Bore x stroke	72 x 100mm
Compression ratio	6.4:1
Power	135hp at 5200rpm
Top speed	99mph
L x W x H	430 x 150 x 135cm
Weight	1500kg
Wheelbase	330cm
Front track width	135cm
Rear track width	135cm
Production date	1934-40 (T57)
Production number	769 (T57)
Original price	FF 60,000-70,000

#205 was most likely exchanged for #49 while the vehicle was in Dovaz's possession. This engine was originally part of the Bugatti, bearing chassis number 57166, which was also owned by Michel Dovaz for some time.

The Bugatti Ventoux during the relocation to Château de Folmont, 1984.
(Courtesy Didier Lainé/Editions LVA)

At the museum in Sarlat, 1989-90.
(Courtesy Editions LVA)

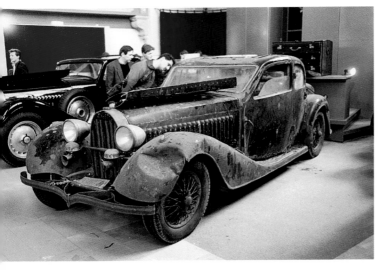

The Ventoux during the auction in Lyon, 1993.
(Courtesy Jaap Braam Ruben Collection)

During the restoration by André LeCoq, 1993-94. As an exhibition item, the car was restored on only the right side at first. (Courtesy Yan Verdier)

Just before its restoration, the Ventoux also made an appearance in a photo-reportage published in a French classic car magazine *Retroviseur*[5]. Against the backdrop of an industrial zone, the Bugatti served as the focal point of the outdoor home of an alcoholic drifter.

André Lecoq subsequently made a showpiece out of the Bugatti, with the object of demonstrating his own skills. Initially, he only restored one side of the vehicle, along a clearly distinguished line from the radiator to the back-end. The result was presented at the Paris Rétromobile Motor Show in 1994.

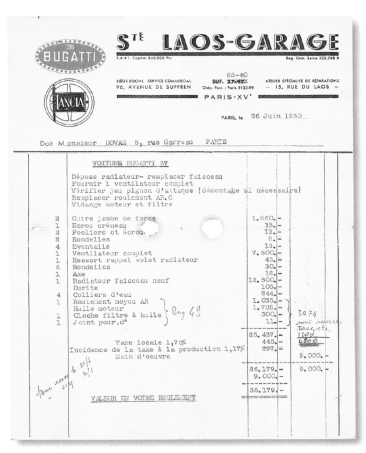

Garage invoice by Sté Laos Garage in Paris, dated 1950. (Courtesy Michel Dovaz)

During restoration of the second half, 1994. (Courtesy André LeCoq)

Restored fifty-fifty at the classic car fair, Rétromobile, in Paris, 1994. (Courtesy André LeCoq)

The other half of the 57 was restored after the show. Once the restoration was complete, Lecoq sold the car to a nephew of French actor and Bugatti enthusiast, Jaques Dufilho. Andre Dulfilho, a surgeon from the North of France, sold the world's most famous 'sleeping beauty' to Karl Ritter from the automobile museum in Stainz, Austria in 2010.

The Bugatti after complete restoration, 2003. (Courtesy André Dufilho)

1936 Bugatti Type 57 Coupé Fontana
Chassis number 57407

This Bugatti has generated quite a bit of confusion. Generally, the vehicle is known to be a 1936 Coupé, featuring a Fontana body on chassis number 57407. However, Dr Pierre Yves Laugier, one of the world's most respected Bugatti experts, is convinced that it is actually a 1935 Gangloff Coupé, with a chassis number close to 57250.

According to Laugier, the real Bugatti 57407 (which is a Van Vooren cabriolet) was also owned by Michel Dovaz, and is still travelling the roads of France today, bearing chassis number 57294. Given that the Coupé described in this section is fitted with the original engine #141 of the 57294, one might assume that the chassis numbers of the two vehicles were mixed up. However, even that would not explain why the elegant coupé has also been linked to a different body shop. So we will have to live with some uncertainty in this context. As both vehicles are covered in this book, we will initially presume

Back view of the Coupé Fontana during the relocation, 1984.
(Courtesy Didier Lainé/Editions LVA)

that a Coupé Fontana with chassis number 57407 does actually exist. The information pertaining to the Bugatti 57294 can be found in the following sections.

The Coupé Fontana during the relocation, 1984. (Courtesy Didier Lainé/Editions LVA)

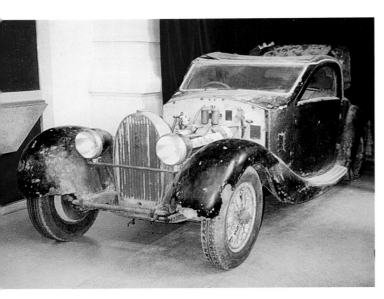

During the auction in Lyon, 1993. (Courtesy Jaap Braam Ruben Collection)

The 'barn find' diorama at the Sarlat museum, 1989-90. (Courtesy Edmund Nankivell)

In still unrestored condition at Henry Novo, 1993. (Courtesy Yan Verdier)

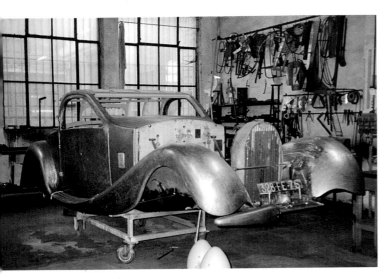

During the restoration in Turin, 1996. (Courtesy Francesco Guasti)

Bugatti Type 57, bearing chassis number 57407, was sold in chassis form to its original owner Vuatine in March 1936. The Coupé body was subsequently added at Fontana in Renens-Vaud, Switzerland. The then owner, had the vehicle repaired at Rogier Teillac in Paris in 1938. It is not known when Michel Dovaz actually acquired the Coupé. However, its outline can be seen in the background in one of the videos recorded at Villemaréchal. It was parked in the half-open barn along with three other Bugattis. At Sarlat, this Type 57 shared a traditional 'barn find' scene with the previously described Type 44. Jean-Michel Bonabosch also bought this Bugatti, which changed hands once again at the 1993 auction in Lyon for a price of FF 850,000. The buyer was probably Italian. In 1996, the Coupé was restored at Novaira in Turin. Unfortunately, it was not possible for us to determine whether the car is still in Italy today.

Technical data: Bugatti Type 57 Coupé Fontana	
Engine	eight-cylinder in-line 3257cc
Bore x stroke	72 x 100mm
Compression ratio	6.4:1
Power	135hp
Top speed	99mph
L x W x H	unknown
Weight	1500kg
Wheelbase	330cm
Front track width	135cm
Rear track width	135cm
Production date	1934-40 (T57)
Production number	769 (T57)
Original price	unknown

1937 Bugatti Type 57 SC Atalante
Chassis number 57542SC

Only 47 of the Jean Bugatti-designed Type 57 Coupé Atalante – which is not to be confused with the even rarer Atlantic – were ever made.

Most of them were built on the lower and shortened 'surbaissé' chassis of the 57S. Only a single car was equipped with a supercharger by the factory as a Type 57SC, however, many of the Type 57S Atalantes were later updated, which boosted their power from 170hp to about 200hp.

The only real Atalante Type 57SC, with chassis number 57542SC, was delivered new to Vidal in Paris in June 1937. Vidal sold the car to Anna Magnin-Dufaux from Versailleux, an heir of the Swiss car manufacturer Dufaux, in December 1938.

Technical data:
Bugatti Type 57 SC Atalante

Engine	eight-cylinder in-line 3257cc
Bore x stroke	72 x 100mm
Compression ratio	unknown
Power	200hp
Top speed	124mph
L x W x H	unknown
Weight	1500kg
Wheelbase	298cm
Front track width.	135cm
Rear track width..	135cm
Production date	1937-38 (T57 SC)
Production number. ..	40 (T57 Atalante)
Original price	unknown

Dovaz's Atalante was the only factory-built SC. (Courtesy Pierre-Yves Laugier and Julius Kruta, 2004)

She hid the car during the war and sold it to a buyer in Colmar in 1948. Michel Poberejsky, from Neuilly, acquired the Atalante (from the Dominique Lamberjack dealership in Paris) in about 1950, for what would, today, have been just a few hundred euros

Poberejsky participated in car races in the 1950s, under the alias Mike Sparken. In 1952, at the Linas-Montlhéry circuit near Paris, Michel Dovaz, with whom he had been friends since boyhood, co-piloted the car. After this race, the Atalante underwent repairs for several months at Lamberjack, because several connecting-rods had been unable to withstand the stress of speeds close to 124mph. In January 1954, Poberejski sold the Atalante to Dovaz, who used it for day-to-day driving in Paris and Geneva for the following four years. Michel Dovaz had the originally free-standing headlights integrated into the front wings.

In 1958, Dovaz began storing the Atalante Coupé in Montlhéry, in a space below an inclined curve at the local race circuit, along with other vehicles.

Six years later, he moved the cars to his new domicile at Villemaréchal, a town south of Paris. The chassis of the Atalante was damaged in transit. Dovaz made vain attempts to repair the car, but when the 'sleeping beauties' were photographed, the disassembled Atalante was still parked in the workshop at his Villemaréchal property.

In 2004, the car was still unrestored.
(Courtesy Pierre-Yves Laugier and Julius Kruta)

At Le Mans, 1958.
(Courtesy Pierre-Yves Laugier and Julius Kruta)

Below the racetrack in Linas-Montlhéry, where the car was stored from 1958 until 1964.
(Courtesy Pierre-Yves Laugier and Julius Kruta)

The Bugatti T57 SC Atalante in Geneva, 1954.
(Courtesy Pierre-Yves Laugier and Julius Kruta)

The Bugatti at the Sarlat museum, being sculptured from stone, 1989-90. (Courtesy **The Automobile***)*

After its appearance in the global press, the Type 57SC became the most glaring victim of the thieves who began to harass Michel Dovaz. They used a welding torch to remove the entire front axle and transmission from the car. At Sarlat, the Atalante was ultimately displayed as a statue created by an ingenious sculptor.

Michel Dovaz appears to have had a very special relationship with this car. Almost adoringly, he calls it "la S". Consequently, it is hardly surprising that he did not give "la S" to just anyone when he sold his collection. Instead, he gave it to his friend, Michel Breuil, from Penne. The latter, however, sold the 57SC to Philippe Salvan soon after, who, like Breuil, did not attempt to restore the Atalante, though did replace all the missing parts. In early 2004, Salvan sold the vehicle to Peter Rae, of Houghton, UK, who commissioned a very careful restoration at the garage of Paul Grist. Every part that could be salvaged was kept intact. As a result, the interior still boasts the original leather, and the paint used was authentic nitrogen paint, which had been used as early as the 1930s.

The 57542SC changed hands again in 2007, when it was sold to an industrial entrepreneur from Germany. The stolen front axle had been installed in a replica of the Type 57 Atlantic for quite some time, and it was not until 2008 that the parts could once again be paired up with the original vehicle. The restored Atalante made its first public appearance at a Bugatti Convention in Badenweiler in Germany's Black Forest in June 2009.

Twelve other Bugattis owned by Dovaz

ରୂଛନ

Besides his nine 'sleeping beauties', Michel Dovaz was, at one time or another, the owner of twelve other Bugattis. However, these vanished from his collection long before 1983.

Some of them were sold earlier, others were stripped for parts, and some were actually scrapped. At least two Bugattis in Dovaz's possession were stolen. A Type 43, which was stolen in 1975, does not exist any longer, at least as far as we know. The other vehicle was stolen from a garage in Porte de Versailles, Paris, in the 1950s. However, the last two owners of the vehicle did at least obtain ownership of the car legally and in good faith.

Before we provide brief descriptions of the other twelve Dovaz Bugattis, we need to make one thing very clear; contrary to rumours that claim otherwise, Michel Dovaz never owned a Bugatti Type 50 Profilée. He did indeed plan to purchase one of these extremely rare cars at one point; however, according to what he told us, the acquisition never materialized.

1914-26 Bugatti Type 27 Brescia
Chassis number 1862

Bugatti's early four-cylinder models (13 to 27) were originally made with 8 valves and later also with 16 valves. Ever since these 16-valve models were placed in the top four at the 1921 Voiturette Grand Prix in Brescia, Italy, they were nicknamed Brescia,

or Brescia modifié models. The company produced a total of about 2000 of these 16-valve models.

Michel Dovaz bought one such Bugatti Type 27 Brescia with chassis number 1862 from Jean Vernhe. Since 1965, this car has been owned by a Frenchman.

Bugatti Type 27 Brescia (#1862) followed by Grand Prix Bugatti Type 35.
(Courtesy Kees Jansen)

1927-31 Bugatti Type 35B

The racing car Bugatti Type 35 quickly reached legendary status, and dominated the Grand Prix circuits of its era. Between 1924 and 1935, about 340 of these cars with different engines were built and sold not only to racing car drivers, but also to the general public. Version Type 35B boasted a 2.3-litre eight-cylinder in-line engine with a supercharger, which developed 140hp.

Michel Dovaz acquired his Bugatti T35B in Paris. He later fitted the engine and wheels of the car to his Bugatti Type 55 Faux Cabriolet. The remainder of this Type 35B was probably destroyed at an early stage.

1926-27 Bugatti Type 38

Touring car Bugatti Type 38 was the less-successful successor of Type 30. It was manufactured from 1926 to 1929, and only 387 units were built.

Michel Dovaz purchased a Bugatti Type 38 from a previous owner by the name of Desjardins. However, he did not take a particular interest in the vehicle, which had a converted two-seater body. He dismantled the car and kept only the engine, drive and the radiator. Later these parts were stolen from his property at Villemaréchal, along with many other components.

A Bugatti T44 cabriolet #441246 in a period photo.
(Courtesy Lionel Decrey)

1927-35 Bugatti Type 43
Chassis number 43158

A total of 160 of these Bugatti Type 43 sports cars were manufactured from 1927-35. The engine was borrowed from the Grand Prix Bugatti Type 35B.

A Monsieur Balleyguier sold the T43 with chassis number 43158 to Michel Dovaz. On February 17, 1975 the Type 43 was stolen from a garage in an eastern suburb of Paris. Its whereabouts are unknown even today.

1930 Bugatti Type 44 Cabriolet
Chassis number 441246

This beautiful four-seater cabriolet was delivered to the Omnium dealership in Epinal, France in September, 1930. The owners who preceded Dovaz included composer Daniel White (*Belle et Sébastien*) and as of 1952, the famous French actor Jacques Dufilho. The car had connecting-rod damage when Michel Dovaz bought it from Dufilho. He had it repaired and sold it to a Paris priest named Marie in 1955. However, it was sold with the registration documents (carte grise) of another Bugatti (chassis number 44801) by mistake. As a result, this Bugatti was known under this incorrect number for a long time. Subsequent owners included Novo, Miss U. Crook (1973-74), Cattaneo, and Rudi Kousbroek.

Today, the 441246 is owned by Lionel Decrey from Switzerland.

The same T44 cabriolet (see previous page) in 2004. (Courtesy Lionel Decrey)

1930-32 Bugatti Type 46 cabriolet
Chassis number 46460

1930 Bugatti Type 49
Chassis number 49161

Given its kinship with the gigantic Type 41 Royale, the Bugatti Type 46 was nicknamed 'the small Royale.' The engine had also been derived from the Royale, whereby the capacity was reduced from an imposing 12.7 litres, to a still impressive 5.3 litres. About 400 Bugattis T46 were made between 1930 and 1932.

Michel Dovaz bought the four-seater T46 cabriolet, with chassis number 46460 from the previous owner named Schriver. According to Dovaz, he eventually scrapped the car.

Chassis 49161 was manufactured in October 1930, and subsequently fitted with a body at Gangloff in Colmar. The exact body model that was fitted is unknown. It was very likely either a closed saloon (Conduite Interieur) or a 'Faux Cabriolet'. The car was delivered to dealership Giraud Hoffman, in January 1931. Michel Dovaz purchased this Bugatti Type 49 in February 1951. Unfortunately, nothing more about the history and fate of this Bugatti is known today.

1930-34 Bugatti Type 49
Chassis number 49197

Chassis number 49197 refers to another Bugatti Type 49, once owned by Michel Dovaz. The previous owner was C Nugue. Nothing more is known about this vehicle.

1934 Bugatti Type 57
Chassis number 57166

This was another factory-made Galibier sedan. This one was identified by chassis number 57166. The car itself, was made and delivered to the "Auto Hall" dealership in Perpignan, in May 1934. The first owner was a man named "Scoiffier." One of the later owners was Michel Dovaz. The original engine #49 of this vehicle was later found in Michel Dovaz's Bugatti Type 57 Ventoux (chassis number 57286). The Galibier was last seen in 1962, at the Garage Hebert, Châteauneuf-en-Thymerais, south of Paris, with a defunct engine. If Dovaz did in fact exchange the engines of the two vehicles, this might have been the original engine #205 removed from the Ventoux. Given that the 57166 subsequently never made another appearance, we consider it safe to assume that the car was destroyed in the 1960s.

1934 Bugatti Type 57 Atalante
Chassis number 57252

This is yet another Atalante, and this one had a standard chassis. The vehicle was manufactured in November 1934, and was shipped to the Monestier dealership in Lyon in May 1935. Michel Dovaz acquired the Type 57 from a Paris-based dealer, Edgar Bensoussan, in December 1950, and sold it to Jean De Dobbeleer in 1956. According to Dovaz, the freestanding headlights were integrated into the front wings only after the sale. The subsequent owners were Greenlee (1957), North (1979), Dixon and Jones. In 1988, the car went to Mr Artom, an Italian. Just a few years ago it was sold to a new owner in England, where the newly-restored car, now sprayed cream and black, once again became available for sale in 2008.

Bugatti T57 Atalante #57252 in England, 2008. (Courtesy Julius Kruta)

1935 Bugatti Type 57 Cabriolet Van Vooren
Chassis number 57294

As previously explained, there has been some confusion relating to chassis numbers 57294 and 57407. Bugatti expert Dr Pierre Yves Laugier presumes that the Bugatti, now known as number 57294, is the real 57407. We were unable to reconcile the contradictions, and have thus decided to describe only chassis number 57294 in this section. Information on chassis number 57407 can be found in the relevant earlier section.

The factory cabriolet, bearing chassis number 57294, was shipped to its original owner, Bourgeois, in January 1935. Consequently, it must have been manufactured prior to March, 1935, as shown in the factory listing. This Bugatti, which is now known to be the 57294, was acquired by Michel Dovaz in September 1956. The list of subsequent owners included Corniere, J Lelievre (1967-75), and Seydoux. The vehicle resurfaced in 1976 at an auction in the French town of Hardelot. Today, it can be found in the South of France, and has a cabriolet body by Van Vooren, which allegedly had originally

been paired with chassis number 57146. Engine #387 which was originally part of 57318, is also installed in the vehicle. The original engine #149 of 57294 can now be found in the Bugatti known as 57407.

Bugatti T57 Cabriolet Van Vooren #57294.
(Courtesy Wilfried Kruse)

1938 Bugatti Type 57 Ventoux
Chassis number 57628

This is yet another, albeit later, version of the Bugatti Type 57 Ventoux. The original owner, Fabre, took delivery of the vehicle in November 1938. This

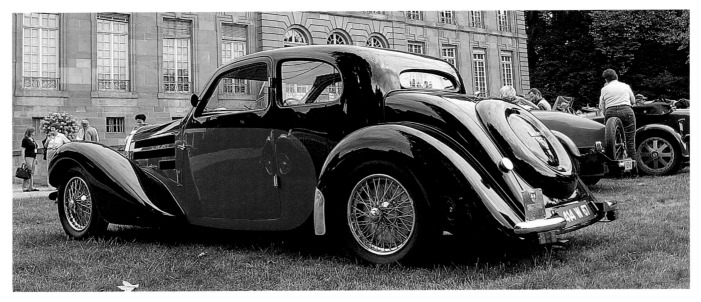

Bugatti T57 Ventoux #57628 in 2005. (Courtesy Nicolas Guhring)

Bugatti T57 Ventoux #57628 in Molsheim, 2006. (Courtesy Nicolas Guhring)

Bugatti was a temporary member of the Dovaz collection as well, possibly during the early 1960s. Frequently referred to as the 'Persillon Bugatti', after one of its previous owners, the black-red vehicle was owned by an Italian named Boldrini in 2003.

In 2005, the Ventoux came up for auction at Poulain le Fur, Paris, and fetched close to €237,000. The car is now owned by a Frenchman, and was seen at the EBA Bugatti Festival, in Molsheim, in 2006.

The nine Lancias

⚮

Talking about his collection and the post-Bugatti era, Michel Dovaz told us, "Après les Bugatti, je roulais les Lancia." (After the Bugattis, I drove Lancias). Back then, he had a thing about Lancia models, which lasted for quite some time. The company had been established in 1906 by Vincenzo Lancia and Claudia Fogolin in Turin, Italy, under the name 'Lancia & C Fabbrica Automobili.' Dovaz owned a total of nine Lancias, all of which were sold to the same Italian buyer when the collection was sold in 1990.

of the Musée de Sarlat placed the Dilambda outdoors in front of the museum, in order to attract attention to the venue. After the museum was closed, the Dilambda remained parked for a short time at the Château de Sanxet, until it could be sold.

Rumour has it that the Dilambda was converted to an open racing car in Italy, so its original body was most probably destroyed.

1929-35 Lancia Dilambda

The oldest Lancia Michel Dovaz ever owned, was a Dilambda. After Lancia's plans to establish a subsidiary in the United States had failed, the prototypes it developed for the US market were introduced at the Paris Motor Show in 1929, as the Lancia Dilambda. Boasting a 100hp V8 engine with almost 4 litres of capacity, the Dilambda was a success. However, with a total of 1686 units built, it fell far short of the sales generated by its predecessor model, the Lambda.

At Villemaréchal, the car had been parked in a corner of the garden along with 14 others, and was barely protected by the open carport. Given that it was already in quite a miserable state, the managers

Technical data:
Lancia Dilambda

Engine .. .. .8-cylinder V 3958cc
Bore x stroke. .. .. .79.37 x 100mm
Compression ratio 5.35:1
Power .. .. .100hp at 4000rpm
Top speed .. .. .unknown
L x W x H .. .. .unknown
Weight .. .. .unknown
Wheelbase .. .. .329cm
Front track width. .. .. .unknown
Rear track width .. .. .. .unknown
Production date 1929-35
Production number. .. .1686
Original price .. .. .unknown

As an outdoor eye-catcher at the Musée de Sarlat, 1989-90. (Courtesy Editions LVA)

The Lancia Dilambda (right) during the relocation to Château de Folmont, 1984.
(Courtesy Didier Lainé/Editions LVA)

1937-39 Lancia Astura Berline Pininfarina

The 4-cylinder Artena and the 8-cylinder Astura were launched in 1931, and lauded as the successors to the Lambda and Dilambda, although the latter continued in production up until 1935. Many of the Asturas were paired with bodies made by the large coachbuilders in Italy and France, however, a few were also completed by less famous coachbuilders, such as Otto Rasch in Germany, or Sodomka in Czecheslovakia. The Austura's V8 engine developed 72hp from 2.6 litres of capacity in the first two series, and 82hp from 3.0 litres in series three and four. The luxurious Astura, of which exactly 2912 units were manufactured between 1931 and 1939,

Technical data:
Lancia Astura Berline

Engine .. ..8-cylinder V 2972cc
Bore x stroke. .. ..75 x 85mm
Compression ratio 5.35:1
Power .. ..82hp at 4000rpm
Top speed 80mph
L x W x H .. ..580 x 165 x 170cm
Weight 1800kg
Wheelbase 347cm
Front track width. 142cm
Rear track width 142cm
Production date .. .. ..1937-39 (fourth series)
Production number. .. ..2912 (Astura 1931-39)
Original price .. ..unknown

During the relocation, 1984. (Courtesy Didier Lainé/Editions LVA)

was popular even among heads of state. Italy's dictator Benito Mussolini, for instance, used a variety of Lancia Asturas as representative government cars, as did his arch-enemy, Haile Selassie, the emperor of Ethiopia.

Michel Dovaz's Astura was probably a specimen of the fourth series with a body by Pininfarina. At Villemaréchal, the Astura stood in a group with the Dilambda, two Lincolns and a Hotchkiss under an open carport. The vehicle was not displayed at Sarlat. Even after 1990, sightings of the unrestored car in Italy were reported, however, that's where the Astura's trail ends.

The Astura in Italy, after 1990.
(Courtesy Dick Janssen)

1951-58 Lancia Aurelia B20 GT

Four Lancias from the Dovaz collection were actually representatives of the Aurelia series, and three of them were B20 GT designs. The Aurelia was designed by Vittorio Jano and was the first car that sported a V6 engine to be launched into the market. The B20 GT Coupé originally developed 75hp from 2.0 litres of capacity, and later 118hp from 2.5 litres. It celebrated victories during several 1950s race events. G Bracco and U Maglioli, for instance, came in second at the 1951 Mille Miglia. The bodies of the almost 4000 B20 GTs that were manufactured during the era were made by Pininfarina, based on a Ghia design.

The whereabouts of the three Dovaz B20 GTs are not known, although it is an established fact that all of the Lancias were sold to Italy in one package, in 1990. They were never displayed at Sarlat, and have disappeared without trace. At Villemaréchal, all three had been stored outdoors, and were in such a miserable state that they probably had only a slim chance of survival. This is a shame, because one of the lost cars was an Aurelia B20 GT with an air intake on the bonnet, which is indicative of a Lusso design, or a later racing conversion. In the book,

Technical data: Lancia Aurelia B20 GT	
Engine	6-cylinder V 2451cc (example)
Bore x stroke	75 x 85.5mm
Compression ratio	8.0:1
Power	118hp at 5000rpm
Top speed	115mph
L x W x H	437 x 155 x 135cm
Weight	1100kg
Wheelbase	266cm
Front track width	128cm
Rear track width	130cm
Production date	1951-58
Production number	Circa 4000
Original price	unknown

Sleeping Beauties [2], one of the three Aurelia B20s is incorrectly identified as an Aurelia D24 Spyder. None of the photos in the book shows this racing version, of which only ten were ever made.

A Lancia Aurelia B20 GT, comparable to the Dovaz model. (Courtesy Jonathan Cence)

1952 Lancia Aurelia B52 Coupé Vignale

Chassis Number B52.1015

The fourth Lancia Aurelia once owned by Michel Dovaz is a much rarer edition, whose destiny was only determined by accident. Author Kay Hottendorff attended the Technoclassica tradeshow in Essen, in March, 2007, and happened to take pictures of many vehicles, including a Lancia Aurelia B52 Coupé sporting a Vignale body. When he later inspected the photos, he found that this vehicle, with chassis number B52.1015 was indeed a car from the Dovaz collection. Of the 98 units of the Aurelia B52 made between 1952 and 53, only two are known to have been bodied by the Italian Carozzeria, Vignale.

Michel Dovaz's Aurelia B52 Vignale Coupé was displayed at the Musée de Sarlat, as part of a fifties-style picnic scene. After the museum was shut down, it was sold to Italy, along with all the other Lancias

Technical data:
Lancia Aurelia B52 Coupé Vignale

Engine	.6-cylinder V 1991cc
Bore x stroke.	.72 x 81mm
Compression ratio	.7.8:1
Power	.70hp at 4800rpm
Top speed	.90mph
L x W x H	.unknown
Weight	.1050kg
Wheelbase	.unknown
Front track width.	.unknown
Rear track width	.unknown
Production date	.1952-53 (B52)
Production number. ..	.98 (B52)
Original price	.unknown

that had been in the collection. In 2002, Paul VJ Koot from the Netherlands purchased the B52 from G Schön, who hailed from Milan, Italy. He displayed

Picnic scene with the Lancia Aurelia B52 Coupé Vignale at the musée de Sarlat, 1989-90.
(Courtesy Didier Lainé)

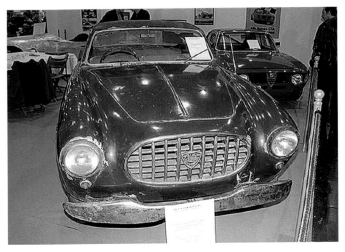

The Lancia still unrestored at the Technoclassica in Essen (D), 2003. (Courtesy Björn Schmidt)

The restored Lancia at the Concourse d'Elégance Palais Het Loo (NL), 2006. (Courtesy Harry Hoving)

At the Technoclassica in Essen (D), 2007. (Hottendorff/op de Weegh)

the unrestored vehicle at the Technoclassica 2003 in Essen. Four years later, the completely restored car resurfaced at the Technoclassica, and was photographed by Kay Hottendorff.

It remains a mystery, why a distinct air inlet, which had not been there before, was inserted into the bonnet of the vehicle during the restoration process. It is possible, that this idea was based on the only other known B52 Vignale (chassis number B52.1026, which at some point had been part of the Blackhawk Collection, USA), which also sports such an air inlet. Dovaz's B52 Coupé was sold upon restoration, and is still in the Netherlands today. At the local Concourse Paleis Het Loo 2006 it made another appearance, and took second place in the Italian Sculptures class.

1957-70 Lancia Flaminia Berlina

Lancia found itself confronted by financial troubles in 1955, which forced the family to sell its stake in the business. The first model to be launched under new proprietor Carlo Pesenti, was the 1957 Flaminia. Although its power had been boosted from 102hp to 128hp, the heavy 4-door Berlina could not compete with other contemporaries, and its sales fell short of expectations.

In 1983, Michel Dovaz's Flaminia Berlina was found in a barn, along with two Cords, three Bugattis and the Alfa 6C 2300. The vehicle is not shown in any of the photos taken at Villemaréchal. It was probably considered a nuisance when the photos of the classic cars from the 30s were taken, and was consequently removed. Ultimately, the existence of the car was confirmed in old video recordings. This Lancia also never made an appearance at Sarlat and once it was sold to Italy, vanished without a trace.

Technical data:
Lancia Flaminia Berlina

Engine	6-cylinder V 2458cc (example)
Bore x stroke	80 x 81.5mm
Compression ratio	8.4:1
Power	110hp at 5200rpm
Top speed	104mph
L x W x H	485.5 x 175 x 148cm
Weight	1510kg
Wheelbase	287cm
Front track width	136.8cm
Rear track width	137cm
Production date	1957-70 (Berlina)
Production number	3943 (Berlina)
Original price	27,000 Gulden (1963)

A similar Lancia Flaminia to the Dovaz model.
(Courtesy Michel Villard)

1957-65 Lancia Flaminia GT Coupé

In addition to building its own Flaminia Berlina sedans, Lancia commissioned other Flaminia versions from outside body shops such as Pininfarina, Zagato and Touring. Thanks to its aluminium body, the Lancia Flaminia GT Coupé by Touring was at a great advantage, in comparison to the Flaminia Berlina, and was known as a much more powerful vehicle. The 2.5-litre V6 engine of the GT developed more than 119hp, and the subsequent 2.8-litre V6 crossed the 150hp threshold. Michel Dovaz owned not one, but two of the 1718 Flamina GTs manufactured between 1957 and 1965. Both were stored outdoors at Villemaréchal, and were not part of the later exhibits at the Musée de Sarlat. They, too, disappeared after they had been sold to an Italian buyer.

Technical data:
Lancia Flaminia GT

Engine .. .. .V6-cylinder 2775cc (example)
Bore x stroke. .. .. .85 x 81.5mm
Compression ratio 9.0:1
Power .. .. .150hp at 5400rpm
Top speed .. .. .120mph
L x W x H .. .. .450 x 166 x 130.5cm
Weight.. .. .. .1360kg
Wheelbase.. .. .. .252cm
Front track width. .. .. .137cm
Rear track width.. .. .. .137cm
Production date 1957-65
Production number. .. .1718 (GT)
Original price .. .. .unknown

One of two Lancia Flamina GTs ready to be relocated to southern France, 1984. (Courtesy Didier Lainé/Editions LVA)

Bella Macchina
– eight sporty Italians

ℭℜℰ𝔒

Auto enthusiasts do not necessarily have a proficient command of the Italian language, but they do understand a number of Italian terms, as they are part of the jargon of the automotive world: "Gran Turismo," "Competizione," "Mille Miglia," ... these words are music to the ears of car buffs. When they dream of Italian sports cars, many instantly think of high speeds, luxury cars, a travel bug and fiery Mediterranean lifestyles. Is there anyone who does not know what people are talking about when they adoringly refer to a car as a "Bella Macchina"? The following eight vehicles from the Dovaz collection have definitely more than earned this honorary title.

1938 Alfa Romeo 6C 2300 B Mille Miglia Touring
Chassis number 815053

The business that Alfa Romeo eventually sprang from was founded as early as 1906 in Milan, by a Frenchman named Alexandre Darracq. In 1925, Alfa Romeo began manufacturing vehicles with six-cylinder in-line engines under the 6C designation. The 2.3-litre 6C 2300 first rolled off the line in 1934. Only 106 of the Mille Miglia version, which developed 95hp and was paired with an aluminium body by Touring, were ever made.

One of the five Alfa Romeos that had once been owned by Michel Dovaz was the 6C 2300 B Mille Miglia with chassis number 815053. In 1946, the vehicle was imported to Switzerland from Italy by a Mr Hoffer, who sold it to Jean-Louis Fatio (CH)

in 1953. Three years later, Dovaz registered it in Switzerland under his name, and in 1958 he did the same in France. At Villemaréchal, the Mille Miglia shared a barn with three Bugattis and two Cords. This was a real privilege, given that it was the most protected storage location on the property. The photos taken in this barn made the 'sleeping beauties' world famous, even though the Alfa was identified as a Fiat 1100 in the book of that title [1].

At Sarlat, the 6C 2300 was shown in a Mille Miglia racing scene. In 1990 it changed hands and was owned by museum founder Thierry Giovannoni, who eventually sold it to Douwe Heida from the Netherlands. The latter restored the car, and gave it a light blue paint job, which, according to Heida, was the original colour as confirmed by Carozzeria Touring. In 1999, Heida won the class victory at the Concourse d'Elegance Paleis Het Loo. He sold the car to Raoul San Giorgi (B), but eventually bought it back. The Alfa was subsequently sold to a German

The Alfa after its arrival in the Netherlands, 1990. (Courtesy Douwe Heida)

Touring Club Suisse . GENÈVE, rue Pierre-Fatio 9 . Tél. 36 60 00
Demande de documents douaniers et de lettre de crédit

Nom ....

Adresse ...... 23 Août 1958

Monsieur DOVAZ Claude

GENÈVE, Rte de Florissant 99

Suisse CH   GE 60811
ALFA ROMEO
815.053
ALFA ROMEO
824.007
    6
    12,44
    Limousine
    ALFA ROMEO
    Bleu ciel
    Cuir rouge
       4
    1938
    1 roue complète
2 phares antibrouillards Marchal
    1400 kgs
    1000.-Frs.ss.

(Ne pas remplir)

Modifications ou adjonctions par rapport à l'ancien document :
....
....

Valeur actuelle en francs suisses ....

TRÈS IMPORTANT. — Prière de joindre la carte de sociétaire valable. Il ne sera donné aucune suite aux demandes de titres qui ne sont pas munies de la signature personnelle du sociétaire.
Les documents ne peuvent être antidatés et doivent être payés à la commande.
Les triptyques exempts de visa doivent être rendus régularisés.

2.101 f

En cas de changement de véhicule veuillez nous remettre le **permis de circulation** et le **passavant suisse.**
Remplir également les rubriques suivantes:

No de sociétaire ....

No de tél. (h. de bureau) ....

Nationalité ....

Lieu de naissance ....
Pour étranger :
No du passeport ....

délivré par ....

le ....

Je désire :
☐ 1 carnet de passages 10 volets
☐ 1 carnet de passages 25 volets
    (valables pour tous les pays)
☐ ou/et triptyque ....
    (valable 1 pays)
☐ 1 triptyque rose pour un seul voyage
☐ 1 carnet à Fr. 500.- de lettre de crédit.

☐ recevoir les documents contre remboursement.
☐ les retirer à vos guichets
✕ Marquer d'une croix la rubrique désirée.

Observations

J'accepte l'engagement situé au verso par l'apposition de ma signature.

.... le .... 19......

Signature : ....

Swiss customs form dated from 1958, referring to the Alfa Romeo 6C 2300 B Mille Miglia. (Courtesy David B Smith)

Technical data:
Alfa Romeo 6C 2300 B Mille Miglia Touring

Engine .. . . .6-cylinder in-line 2309cc
Bore x stroke . . . . .70 x 100mm
Compression ratio 7.75:1
Power .. . .95hp at 4500rpm
Top speed 90mph
L x W x H .. . . .64 x 168 x 155cm
Weight.. . . . . .1380kg
Wheelbase.. . . . . .300cm
Front track width.. . . ..140cm
Rear track width.. . . ..147cm
Production date 1934-39
Production number.. ..106
Original price .. . .unknown

The Alfa after arrival in The Netherlands, 1990. (Courtesy Douwe Heida)

Photos of the relocation show the alloy body in a bad condition, 1984.
(Courtesy Didier Lainé/Editions LVA)

In Sarlat, the Alfa was displayed in a 'Mille Miglia' scene, 1989-90. (Courtesy **The Automobile***)*

investor, via Paul Koot (NL), and in 2002, via Raoul San Giorgi to David B Smith in the United States. The latter restored the vehicle completely, and had it painted black. At the 2007 Concourse d'Elegance in Pebble Beach, California, the Mille Miglia received 100 out of 100 points and was lauded best of its class. Just a year later, it was auctioned off at Pebble Beach where it fetched nearly USD 2.6 million.

In original blue colour scheme, approved by Touring, at the end of the 1990s. (Courtesy Douwe Heida)

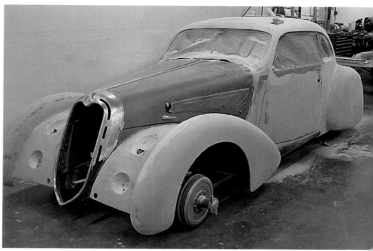

During the second restoration in Seattle, 2005. (Courtesy David B Smith)

After restoration the Alfa 6C 2300 B Mille Miglia wins its class in Pebble Beach, 2007. (Courtesy David B Smith)

1948 Alfa Romeo 6C 2500 Competizione

Chassis number 920002

In 1938, the 6C 2300 was replaced by the 6C 2500, which had nearly 2.5 litres of capacity. During World War II, production ceased almost entirely, and did not begin again until 1946. The most popular body designs today are the Freccia d'Oro and the Villa d'Este.

The power of the 6C 2500 ranged from 87hp in the basic version, to 145hp in the two-seater Competizione racing version, which, thanks to its aluminium body, weighed in at just 850kg. Only three of the 2591 6C 2500s built were actually Competiziones, and, for a long time, Michel Dovaz's car was considered the only survivor of these three. Today, the fate of the two other Competiziones is a matter of much controversy, so we will limit our description to the vehicle bearing chassis number 920002, which was a part of the Dovaz collection. It was made in 1948, and participated in various races, with Franco Rol at the wheel in the Targa Florio, among others. It also competed in the Mille Miglia four times. During 1949, in one of the latter races, Rol and his co-driver, Richiero, achieved third place with the Competizione bearing start number 648. That same year, the pair won the Coppa Acerbo in Pescara. In 1951, the Competizione was imported into Switzerland from Italy by Mr Hoffer, and subsequently changed owners at brief intervals several times thereafter. The owners were Denis Spagnol, Jean Charles Munger, racing driver Gérard Pitet and, finally, in November 1954, Michel Dovaz.

The front end of the Alfa had been modified many times since the Rol era. A photo taken in Monza in the mid-1950s shows the car in a wretched condition with a converted front, air inlet in the bonnet, and a broken-down roof. When it was found in the Dovaz half-open barn at Villemaréchal in 1983, the car once again sported a different front end. At the time, Alfa expert and collector, Guido Bartolomeo, had for some 15 years been trying to convince his

Technical data:
Alfa Romeo 6C 2500 Competizione

Engine	6-cylinder in-line 2443cc
Bore x stroke	72 x 100mm
Compression ratio	9.2:1
Power	145hp at 5500rpm
Top speed	124mph
L x W x H	unknown
Weight	850kg
Wheelbase	250cm
Front track width	135cm
Rear track width	130cm
Production date	1946-1950
Production number	3
Original price	unknown

During the first restoration in 1984: without paintwork, and with non-original front. (Courtesy Het Klaverblaadje)

friend, Michel Dovaz, to sell him the Competizione. However, it was not until shortly after worldwide publication of the photos from Dovaz's garden, in 1983, that Bartolomeo ultimately prevailed and was able to at least talk Dovaz into having the car restored. The project was sponsored by Alfa Romeo France and the French Alfa Romeo Club, and the restoration was assigned to the Alfa Romeo branch in Narbonne. The original front end was rebuilt

Rol and Richiero at the Mille Miglia of 1949.
(Courtesy Corrado Millanta Archive)

Registration card of Rol and Richiero for the Mille Miglia, 1949, where
they came third with the Competizione. (Courtesy David B Smith)

In the 1950s, in Monza, with damaged roof, and modified front.
(Courtesy Rudi Rutz/via Het Klaverblaadje)

93

The Competizione's chassis during the second restoration in Germany, 1997. (Courtesy David B Smith)

Presentation of the first restored 'sleeping beauty' in Linas-Montlhéry, 1984. (Courtesy Dominique Delcros Archive)

The Alfa was the only restored car in Sarlat, 1989-90. (Courtesy Dominique Delcros Archive)

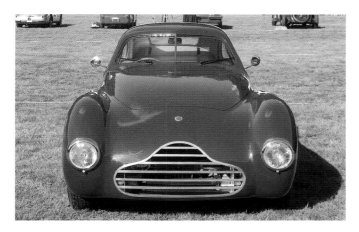

At the Concourse d'Elégance Paleis Het Loo (NL), 2003. (Courtesy Martijn Kaman)

Owner David B Smith (dark blazer) with #920002 in Pebble Beach, California, 2005. (Courtesy Michael T Lynch Archive)

based on photos, and the technical components were updated. The car was also repainted. The damaged bonnet was replaced by the customized fibreglass roof of a Citroën ID19. The interior of the car remained largely unrestored.

Dovaz and Bartolomeo participated in the Mille Miglia with the Alfa Romeo, as early as 1984. The following year, Alfa expert Ben Hendriks (NL) paid Bartolomeo a visit. At the time, the Competizione was stored on the latter's property. In April 1988, the Alfa was briefly displayed at Thierry Giovannoni's Salon de la voiture ancienne collection et prestige, in Bordeaux. Subsequently, it was transferred to the storage location of Dovaz's other cars at the Château de Folmont, where Dorien Berteletti had the opportunity to view it four months later. A year later, the Alfa and 25 other unrestored cars were taken to the Musée de Sarlat. After the museum was closed in 1990, the Alfa went into storage at the Château de Sanxet. In 1995, Raoul San Giorgi (B) purchased the vehicle and sold it to Nicholas Springer (D), who subjected it to a second restoration in Germany. When Springer sold his collection, San Giorgi repurchased the Competizione and continued the restoration process in Milan. The result was presented in 2003 at three major events: the Concourse Villa d'Este (I), the Louis Vuitton Classic, in Paris, and at the Concourse Paleis Het Loo (NL). Shortly thereafter, the current owner, David B Smith (USA) acquired the vehicle. He also procured the original parts that had been replaced during the previous restorations and commissioned another restoration of the Competizione. Today, the front end, bonnet and rear end have all been replaced. The remainder of the body is still original, as is a large portion of the interior and the frame. The vehicle once again has its original engine, and even the first road registration of Franco Rol is still on hand. Today, the car is in its original 1949 configuration – as confirmed by the impressive 100 points the car was awarded in 2005 at Pebble Beach, where it won second place in the Postwar Alfa Sports Racing class.

Incidentally, a 1:43 scale model of this very vehicle is available; it depicts the car with the start number 648, assigned to Franco Rol in 1949.

1950 Alfa Romeo 6C 2500 SS Cabriolet Worblaufen

It is highly likely that only a single version of this 6C 2500 cabriolet by Swiss body shop Worblaufen was ever made. In vehicles with the short Supersport (SS) chassis, the 2.5-litre engine usually developed 105hp.

At Villemaréchal, the car was stored in a closed barn between the second 6C 2500 SS cabriolet in the collection, and one of the two Aston Martin DB2s. It was last seen in 1988 by Dorien Bertletti, in a barn near the Château de Folmont, and was never displayed at the Musée de Sarlat. Michel Dovaz sold the car to a buyer from the Côte d'Azur. Rumours have it that the vehicle is still located in the vicinity of Cannes today, however, unfortunately, further details are not known.

**Technical data:
Alfa Romeo 6C 2500 SS
Cabriolet Worblaufen**

Engine .. .. .6-cylinder in-line 2443cc
Bore x stroke . .. .72 x 100mm
Compression ratio 7.5:1
Power .. ..105hp at 4800rpm
Top speed .. .. .103mph
L x W x H .. ..458 x 178 x 150cm
Weight 1420kg
Wheelbase 270cm
Front track width. 146cm
Rear track width .. .. .. .148cm
Production date .. .. .. .1950
Production number. 1
Original price .. ..unknown

The 6C2500 SS Cabriolet Worblaufen in the early 1950s. (Courtesy Urs Paul Ramseier/Swiss Car Register Archive)

At the Geneva Motor Show, 1950. (Courtesy Urs Paul Ramseier/Swiss Car Register Archive)

1943 Alfa Romeo 6C 2500 SS Cabriolet Touring
Chassis number 915527

Based on the information available, only three 6C 2500 SS cabriolets with Superleggera aluminium bodies by Touring ever appeared. All of the remaining cabriolets in the series came almost exclusively from Pininfarina.

The lines on the side of the vehicle with this chassis number reflect the design of the pre-war 6C 2500, while the front end reflects the postwar design. This was a kind of transition vehicle, which was made in 1943, but was not delivered to the buyer, Count Gourgaud de Tallis, Yerres (CH), until 1945, on account of the war.

Although this Alfa had been housed in a closed dry barn at Villemaréchal, its condition left much to be desired. The impression was further amplified, by apparent crash damage at the front. At the Musée

Technical data:
Alfa Romeo 6C 2500 SS Cabriolet Touring

Engine .. .. .6-cylinder in-line 2443cc
Bore x stroke . . . . .72 x 100mm
Compression ratio 7.5:1
Power .. .. .105hp at 4800rpm
Top speed .. .. .106mph
L x W x H .. ..458 x 178 x 150cm
Weight 1270kg
Wheelbase .. .. .270cm
Front track width . .. .. .146cm
Rear track width .. .. .. .148cm
Production date .. .. .. .1943 (#915.527)
Production number. .. .3
Original price .. .. .unknown

de Sarlat, the Touring cabriolet was displayed in a garage scene dating back to the fifties, along with the silver-grey Aston Martin DB2. After the museum

The Alfa Romeo 6C 2500 Cabriolet Touring at the Sarlat museum, 1989-90. (Courtesy Edmund Nankivell)

The restored Alfa during the Coppa Milano-San Remo in Italy, 2006. (Courtesy Björn Schmidt)

closed, the vehicle was sold to Henri Lalane. In the 1990s, Italian owner, Vittorio Serventi, commissioned the complete restoration of the Alfa. The result was shown in 2002 at the Louis Vuitton Classic in Paris, and the following year at the Concorso d'Eleganza Villa d'Este in Italy. It made another appearance in 2005, at the Technoclassica in Essen (D). Up to mid-2007, several dealerships offered the car for sale. One of the dealers assured researchers that the 915527 did not come from the Dovaz collection. Given that the remaining vehicles have a slightly different design, this would have meant that the Dovaz car was a fourth, previously unknown Cabriolet Touring. We later received a confirmation that the 915527 was indeed the car that had once belonged to Michel Dovaz. The fact that this car was delivered to Switzerland when it was new, and that it was not restored until the 1990s in Italy, confirms this identification.

In the 1960s, Dovaz owned a third 6C 2500 cabriolet. This vehicle, which sported a Pininfarina body, was however no longer part of the collection in 1983.

1951 Ferrari 340 America Berlinetta Ghia
Chassis number 0148A

The Ferrari 340 America in Villemaréchal, 1964-65. (Courtesy Michel Pfau)

Although he had already won acclaim in the 1930s, as part of the Scuderia Ferrari racing team, Enzo Ferrari, an Italian, did not build his first vehicle in his own name until 1947. Three years later, the Ferrari 340 America – of which only 23 units were built until production ended in 1953 – was launched. This model, which was paired with bodies by Touring, Vignale and Ghia, boasted the legendary 4.1-litre 220hp V12 engine, by Lampredi.

Michel Dovaz's 340 America, with chassis number 0148A, has one of only four Ghia Berlinetta bodies, and is probably the only one made of aluminium. Unlike most of the 340s, this vehicle never participated in a race. It was built for French industry magnate Michel Paul Cavalier, even though the flyer published by the Musée de Sarlat incorrectly states that Prince Rainier of Monaco was the first owner. Dovaz bought the Ferrari at a garage in Levallois. The previous owner was a member of the US military, who participated in drag races in a Mercedes Benz 300 SL.

The Ferrari 340 America in Sarlat, with battered chrome and paintwork, 1989-90. (Courtesy Didier Lainé)

Above and below: At the Cavallino Classics, Palm Beach, USA, in race trim without bumpers, 2003. (Courtesy Edvar van Daalen)

The Lampredi V12 after the first restoration of 1999, photo taken in 2003. (Courtesy Edvar van Daalen)

Dovaz stored both of his Ferraris outside at Villemaréchal. A video dating back to about 1964, shows the red 340 at Villemaréchal in the same location where it was found in 1983. The paintwork and chrome elements had already sustained substantial damage when the vehicle was displayed at Sarlat, in a setting reminiscent of an ancient temple. From late 1990, the Ferrari was temporarily housed at the Château de Sanxet, until Dovaz sold the car to a doctor from Paris. Paul Koot (NL) subsequently purchased the Ferrari from the doctor. Koot commissioned a complete restoration of the car with Zagato. Michel Magnin, overhauled the engine, while aluminium body restoration expert, Galbiati, handled the bodywork. In 1999, the Ferrari, which now sported blue paintwork, driven by Marc Souvrain, participated in the Mille Miglia. One year later the 340 was offered for sale by Paris auctioneer Poulain

**Technical data:
Ferrari 340 America Berlinetta Ghia**

Engine	12-cylinder V 4102cc
Bore x stroke	80 x 68.1mm
Compression ratio	8.0:1
Power	220hp at 6000rpm
Top speed	149mph
L x W x H	unknown
Weight	1202kg
Wheelbase	242cm
Front track width	127.8cm
Rear track width	125cm
Production date	1950-53
Production number	12
Original price	unknown

le Fur, but failed to find a buyer. In 2001, the Ferrari was auctioned off by Christie's, during the Concourse d'Elegance at Pebble Beach, for USD 391,000.

The new owner, a US businessman and Ferrari collector, used the car for several years, during which time, he participated in classic car races. He finally decided to have it restored to its original condition, as an on-road vehicle. Today, the Ferrari boasts black paintwork. In 2008 at Pebble Beach it was placed second in its class, gaining 100 points.

The Lampredi V12 after the second restoration, 2008. (Courtesy Dennis Coleman)

Above and below: Restored to original condition as road vehicle (eg with bumpers) after the Concourse d'Elegance in Pebble Beach, 2008. (Courtesy Dennis Coleman)

1962 Ferrari 250 GTE 2+2 Coupé Pininfarina
Chassis number 4227GT

Michel Dovaz's second Ferrari was a 250 GTE 2+2, one of the first Ferraris manufactured in a series that had 2+2 seating. About 955 of these cars were built between 1960 and 1963 at Pininfarina, making the 250 GTE 2+2 a true bestseller. The rated power of the ultra lightweight 3.0-litre V12 GTE 2+2 by Colombo was 240hp. Dovaz's model with chassis number 4227GT stemmed from the third series and was built in 1962. The name of the original owner was Arco. At Villemaréchal, this Ferrari, too, had been stored outside and completely unprotected. The vehicle was never displayed at the Musée de Sarlat, and its current whereabouts are unknown.

The *Sleeping Beauties* book[2] makes incorrect reference to two Ferrari 250s; however, all published photos clearly show only one vehicle.

Technical data:
Ferrari 250 GTE 2+2 Coupé Pininfarina

Engine	.12-cylinder V 2953cc
Bore x stroke	.73 x 58.8mm
Compression ratio	.8.8:1
Power	.240hp at 7000 rpm
Top speed	.143mph
L x W x H	.470 x 171 x 134cm
Weight	.1450kg
Wheelbase	.260cm
Front track width	.139.5cm
Rear track width	.139cm
Production date	.1960-63
Production number	.955
Original price	.unknown

Michel Dovaz's Ferrari 250 GTE belonged to the third series, seen here during the relocation in 1984. (Courtesy Didier Lainé/Editions LVA)

1954 Siata 208 CS Coupé Balbo
Chassis number CS074

Technical data:
Siata 208 CS Coupé

Engine	8-cylinder V 1996cc (example)
Bore x stroke	72 x 61mm
Compression ratio	7.5:1
Power	106hp at 6000rpm
Top speed	112mph
L x W x H	460 x 165 x 145cm
Weight	1120kg
Wheelbase	270cm
Front track width	129cm
Rear track width	129cm
Production date	1952-54
Production number . ..	54
Original price	unknown

Siata, a Turin-based company, founded in 1926 by Giorgio Ambrosiani, originally sold racing sports conversions of Fiats. Later on, the company also introduced a few models of its own into the market, all based on Fiat technology. This was also true for Model 208, Siata's version of the Fiat 8V. The revamped 2.0-litre Fiat V8 engine, developed 106hp. Many of these 54 Siata 208s – which were built between 1952 and 1954 and which sported aluminium bodies – were used in racing events. The Spyder design variations were mostly fitted with bodies by Carozzeria Rocco Motto of Turin, which was a sub-contractor of Vignale and Bertone. The coupés were originally made at Stabilimenti Farina, but production moved to Balbo in 1952.

Michel Dovaz's Siata 208 was a red Coupé Balbo, with chassis number CS074. The vehicle had been sold to Rene Vosser from Baden (CH) in 1954. The subsequent owners were Rodolf Ricky-Frey from Olten (CH) and, in 1958, Hermann Wackerle from Merlischachen (CH), from whom Dovaz eventually purchased the car. At Villemaréchal, the front end of the Siata had substantial paint damage, and its grille was missing. Michel Dovaz told us that these were traces of one of the very few accidents that he had ever had. With a view to repairing the car one day, Dovaz had parked it in a dry and closed garage at Villemaréchal. His appreciation of this car is also evident, from the fact that the Siata was one of only

The partly-restored Siata 208 CS Coupé before 1993. (Courtesy Dirk Libeert)

During the restoration in Italy, 2001-05.
(Courtesy Dirk Libeert)

Above and below: After the restoration, 2007.
(Courtesy Dirk Libeert)

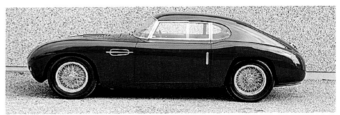

two vehicles that were at least partially renovated, while he owned them. Nonetheless, the Siata never made it into the Musée de Sarlat. At the end of 1990, it was purchased by Giancarlo Mercurio (I), who placed the Siata with a restoration expert. In 1998, the car changed hands and ownership was transferred to Ralph Bruggmann (CH). Two years later, it was registered in the name of Filippo Milesi (I). Since June, 2001, the coupé has been in the possession of Dirk Libeert (B), who commissioned its complete restoration in Italy (completed in 2005). During the restoration process, residue of the original dark red paint, which was discovered on the dashboard, was used as a sample for a respray. However, Libeert was unhappy with the outcome of the restoration, and recently had the Siata restored again, to ensure that it was 100 per cent identical with its original 1954 condition.

The Siata in Belgium, 2007. (Courtesy Dirk Libeert)

1967 Maserati Quattroporte race track fire engine

The company, which was established by the Maserati brothers in 1926, introduced its first four-door sports saloon, the Quattroporte, in 1963. These V8s developed 260hp from 4.1 litres and, as of 1968, 295hp from 4.7 litres. Five of 730 Quattroporte I models built until 1969, were converted into racetrack fire engine cars by Italian fire extinguisher manufacturer CEA. A fire extinguisher cannon, with a foam tank was installed on the loading area of these Maserati pickups. The converted car was also equipped with fire hoses, and fire extinguishers. On the circuits of the 1970s, the five Maseratis were soon known as the world's fastest fire engines.

Guido Bartolomeo eventually purchased all five of these Maseratis, and sold one to Michel Dovaz. This probably didn't happen until after the mid-80s, given that the Maserati does not appear in any of the numerous photos taken at Villemaréchal. The fate of the vehicle is a mystery. Recently, one of the five was available for sale, but it was not the one once owned by Dovaz.

Technical data:
Maserati Quattroporte I

Engine	8-cylinder V 4136cc
Bore x stroke	88.0 x 85.0cm
Compression ratio	8.5:1
Power	260hp at 5600rpm
Top speed	143mph
L x W x H	500 x 172 x 136cm
Weight	1750kg
Wheelbase	275cm
Front track width	139cm
Rear track width	140cm
Production date	1963-69
Production number	Circa 730
Original price	unknown

Maserati Quattroporte race track fire engine: this is a comparable car to Dovaz's.
(Courtesy Christoph Grohe)

Untouched – ten beauties at the Château de Sanxet

⊰⊱

The one travel destination we recommend most highly to fans of the 'sleeping beauties' is the Château de Sanxet, owned by Bertrand de Passemar and his wife, Sabine. The privately-owned, wine-growing estate near Pomport in the Pèrigord (www.sanxet.com – excellent wines!) houses ten of the unrestored automobiles owned by Michel Dovaz. He is still the owner of eight of these, only the two Cords were eventually owned by de Passemar.

Above and opposite: The exhibition hall of the car museum at Château de Sanxet, 2007.
(Hottendorff/op de Weegh)

Nine of the 'sleeping beauties' are displayed in a private museum run by the de Passemars, along with some 25 other vehicles. These nine cars have been carefully conserved, by tending to the corroded areas, and by adding matching colours to the paintwork. Anyone who wants to see the tenth 'sleeping beauty',

will have the feeling of travelling back in time to Dovaz's barns at Villemaréchal. The Tatra 600 Tatraplan has been parked in an ancient barn off to the side since 1990. It has remained untouched, and stands there in the company of other classic cars. An amazing 'barn find'!

1936-39 Panhard & Levassor Dynamic Coupé Major

Panhard & Levassor was one of the world's oldest automobile makers, and launched the first French car onto the market in 1890. The 1936 Dynamic was exceptional in many respects. On the one hand, it was the last model that had the virtually silent sleeve-valve engine, which had been used by Panhard & Levassor since 1910. On the other hand, the Dynamic also made its mark thanks to its streamlined art deco body, designed by Louis Bionier. The Dynamic had covered wheel wells, a three-part panoramic windscreen and grille-covered integrated headlights. The steering wheel was positioned in the centre of the dashboard. This unique design, and the worldwide economic crisis, kept the number of Dynamics

Technical data:
Panhard & Levassor Dynamic Coupé Major

Engine	6-cylinder in-line 2516cc (example)
Bore x stroke	75 x 108mm
Compression ratio	unknown
Power	75hp at 3800rpm
Top speed	80mph
L x W x H	475 x 260 x 142cm
Weight	1800kg
Wheelbase	unknown
Front track width	unknown
Rear track width	unknown
Production date	1936-39
Production number	2742
Original price	unknown

In Sarlat, the Dynamic was placed next to a Lincoln, 1989-90. (Courtesy Didier Lainé)

The Panhard behind the Cord 812 during the relocation, 1984.
(Courtesy Didier Lainé/Editions LVA)

manufactured by 1939 down to a mere 2742. The car was available with three different engine versions, ranging from 75 to 105hp and from 2.5 to 3.8 litres. A variety of body styles were also paired with the chassis. Michel Dovaz's Dynamic was one of the larger of the two available coupés, a Coupé Major. By 1983, the car was already in a rather dilapidated condition, as it had been housed in a barn with a leaky roof. After having been displayed at Sarlat, the Panhard was moved to Château de Sanxet, where all the rust was removed, and it was painted with base coat. However, the interior is still in such a bad shape, that it would make most car enthusiasts cry!

The interior is in really bad condition. Clearly visible is the centrally mounted steering wheel, 2007. (Hottendorff/op de Weegh)

The sleeve valve engine of the Dynamic, 2007. (Hottendorff/op de Weegh)

Completely de-rusted and in prime coat, at Château de Sanxet, 2007. (Hottendorff/op de Weegh)

1950 Jowett Jupiter Coupé Ghia Suisse
Chassis number E0SA56R

Jowett, a British company, built its first car as early as 1910. The first post-World War II model was the streamlined Javelin saloon, which was complemented, as of 1950, by the sporty Jupiter. With its 1.5-litre, flat-four engine, the Jupiter developed 60 and later 63hp, and was the last model to roll off the production line at Jowett.

In 1954, Jowett moved over to manufacturing aircraft components. The chassis was the work of Dr Robert Eberan-Eberhorst, who was responsible for the design of the 1938 Auto Union 'Silberpfeil' Type D. Despite three class victories at Le Mans, 1950-51-52, and at the 1951 Monte Carlo and Lisbon rallies, the Jupiter had limited sales, with just 900 units sold (in comparison to 23,000 Javelins).

Jowett provided 825 of its Jupiters with three-seater open touring bodies. The remaining 75 chassis were out-sourced to coachbuilders. Only two of the

Technical data:
Jowett Jupiter Ghia Suisse

Engine	4-cylinder flat 1486cc
Bore x stroke.	.72.5 x 90mm
Compression ratio	.8.0:1
Power	.60hp at 4750rpm
Top speed	.84mph
L x W.	.426.7 x 157cm
Weight	.900kg
Wheelbase	.236.2cm
Front track width.	.132.1cm
Rear track width	.128.3cm
Production date	.1950-1954 (Jupiter)
Production number. ..	.3 (Jupiter Ghia Suisse)
Original price	.unknown

Jupiters that were fitted with bodies in Switzerland have survived.

The Jupiter with chassis number E0SA56R was manufactured in 1950, and was sent to the Ghia

The Jowett Jupiter in a comic scene at the Sarlat museum, 1989-90. (Courtesy Didier Lainé)

company in Aigle, Switzerland, for pairing with its body in 1951 (this company should not be confused with Ghia, based in Turin, Italy). The customer who commissioned the body was Geneva-based Jowett representative Henri Ziegler. He registered the Coupé, which sported green paintwork at the time, for the Evian-Mont Blanc Rally in July 1951, but failed to show up for the event. Michel Dovaz later acquired this Jupiter model. At Villemaréchal the vehicle, which was now resprayed red, was stored in a barn that was open on one side along with the Bugatti Type 44 and the Alfa Romeo Competizione. This poor storage is evident in the fact that the front end still has substantial rust damage. At Sarlat, the car was displayed with Tintin, hero of the *Tintin & Snowy* comics created by Belgian artist Hergé, behind the steering wheel. The Tintin doll is still sitting in the same spot today, except that the car has since found a home at the Château de Sanxet.

At Château de Sanxet, 2007. (Hottendorff/op de Weegh)

At Château de Sanxet, 2007. (Hottendorff/op de Weegh)

Comic-book hero Tintin at the wheel of the Jupiter at Sanxet, 2007. (Hottendorff/op de Weegh)

1957-62 Lotus Elite

British engineer and designer, Colin Chapman, founded the Lotus company in 1952, and subsequently made cars for both road use and racing. The Lotus Elite, which was rolled out in 1957, was the world's first vehicle with a self-supporting fibreglass body. Weighing in at only 500kg, a total of 998 of these two-seater coupés were manufactured up to 1962. The 1.2-litre four-cylinder in-line engine, made completely of aluminium by Coventry-Climax, developed 75hp in the road version and 105hp in the racing version. The road version of the Lotus Elite was also successful on several circuits, as confirmed by dual class victories at Le Mans in 1961 and 1963.

Michel Dovaz owned two Lotus Elites, one in dark green and one in red. The red version, which had chassis number 1012, was one of the first fourteen Elite models (chassis numbers 1001 to 1014), which were considered factory prototypes. At Villemaréchal, this prototype was completely exposed to the elements, without any protection, as it was parked

Technical data: Lotus Elite	
Engine	.4-cylinder in-line 1216cc (example)
Bore x stroke.	.76.2 x 66.6mm
Compression ratio	.10:1
Power	.75hp at 6100rpm
Top speed	.118mph
L x W x H	.366 x 147 x 117cm
Weight	.559kg
Wheelbase	.223.5cm
Front track width.	.119.3cm
Rear track width..	.119.3cm
Production date	.1957-62
Production number. ..	.988
Original price	.unknown

outside, while the dark green Lotus was housed in the dry garage along with the Bugatti Type 57 Atalante. The red car had been used as a source of parts, and as a result had also switched engines with the dark

Both Lotus cars (here the red one) and an Aston Martin formed a race diorama in Sarlat, 1989-90. (Courtesy Dominique Delcros Archive)

green car. This can probably be attributed to the fact that Coventry-Climax stopped supplying spare parts for the engines at an early stage. Together with an Aston Martin DB2, the two Elites were displayed in a contemporary racing scene at the Musée de Sarlat. Fans can now admire the dark green vehicle at Château de Sanxet. It is still equipped with the engine and carburettors of the red model. Dovaz sold the latter in 1990. Rumour has it that it is somewhere in Belgium these days.

The green Lotus is placed next to the Jowett at Sanxet, 2007. (Hottendorff/op de Weegh)

1929 Cord L-29 Sedan
Chassis number 2928249

To close the price gap between the Auburn and the Duesenberg, Erret Lobban Cord used his own name for a competitive marque, and launched the Cord L-29 in 1929. The innovative L-29 was the first series manufactured car with front -wheel-drive. This technology did not actually begin to penetrate the automotive world until the 1980s. The 4.9-litre, 8-cylinder, in-line engine by Lycoming initially developed 125 and later 130hp. Given that conditions were as tough as they could have been during the stock market crash and the Great Depression, only about 5000 of these cars were made up until 1931.

Michel Dovaz's two Cords were housed in a barn at Villemaréchal, along with three Bugattis and an Alfa Romeo. The photos taken of the 'sleeping beauties' made it the world's most recognized barn in automotive history. Covered by a thick layer of dust, the L-29 appeared beyond restoration at the time. However, when the two Cords reemerged in the James Dean movie backdrop at Sarlat, the amazingly good condition of the L-29 became apparent.

The movie backdrop at the Sarlat museum, 1989-90. (Courtesy Edmund Nankivell)

Unfortunately, the Cord became the victim of a negligent museum guard, who shut his dog in it one day. The dog couldn't have cared less about the car's classic status and slit open the seats, which until then had been well preserved. Other than that, the Cord is still in good condition and is now displayed at the Château de Sanxet, in its original state, covered with a magnificent patina. And yes, the engine still turns over.

The Cord L-29 during the relocation to southern France, 1984. (Courtesy Didier Lainé/Editions LVA)

Technical data:
Cord L-29 Sedan

Engine . . . . .8-cylinder in-line 4888cc
Bore x stroke . . . . .82.6 x 114.3mm
Compression ratio 5.3:1
Power . . . . .125hp at 3400rpm
Top speed 77mph
L x W x H . . . . .unknown
Weight 2041.2kg
Wheelbase 349.3cm
Front track width 147.3cm
Rear track width 152.4cm
Production date 1929-31
Production number . . . .Circa 5000 (L-29)
Original price . . . . .unknown

Cord L-29 with wonderful patina at Château de Sanxet, 2007. (Hottendorff/op de Weegh)

1937 Cord 812 Supercharged Custom Berline

Chassis number 310132B

The streamlined design of the Cord 810/812 was the brainchild of Gordon M. Buehrig, and caused quite a stir at the 1935 US auto shows. Even today, collectors consider it one of the most beautiful cars ever made. This car also sported front-wheel-drive and was the first to have turning, wheel-operated, folding headlights. Buehrig simply borrowed the landing lights from aeronautics subsidiary Stinson Aircraft. The 4.7-litre Lycoming V8 was optionally available with a supercharger as of 1937, and, subsequently, was meant to develop 170 instead of 125hp, but it did in fact often develop 195hp. Buyers loved the

Technical data:
Cord 812 Supercharged Custom Berline

Engine .. .. .8-cylinder V 4729cc
Bore x stroke. .. .. .88.90 x 95.30mm
Compression ratio.. .. .6.5:1
Power .. .. .170hp at 3600rpm
Top speed .. .. .110mph
L x W. .. .. .480.1 x 195.6cm
Weight.. .. .. .1775.8kg
Wheelbase.. .. .. .335.3cm
Front track width. 142.2cm
Rear track width.. .. .. .154.9cm
Production date .. .. .. .1937
Production number. .. .11 (812 Custom Berline)
Original price .. .. .unknown

*The Cord 812 at the Sarlat museum, 1989-90.
(Courtesy Edmund Nankivell)*

*During the relocation, 1984.
(Courtesy Didier Lainé/Editions LVA)*

Both Cords during arrival at Château de Sanxet, 1990. (Courtesy Bertrand de Passemar)

The streamlined Cord, designed by Gordon Buehrig, in the automobile museum at Château de Sanxet, 2007. (Hottendorff/op de Weegh)

Cord 810/812. However, it encountered significant technical problems (eg with the highly complex transmission), so it did not become the huge success it could have been. Close to 3000 Cord 810/812 cabriolets, and sedans were made before the Auburn, Cord and Duesenberg makes vanished from the market in 1937.

Michel Dovaz's model 812 was one of only eleven Custom Berlines ever made, identified as such by its chauffeur features and retractable partition. With its shattered windscreen, hooded headlights, and covered by a thick layer of dust, the Cord looked just as picturesque at Villemaréchal as its famous neighbour, the Bugatti Type 57 Ventoux. The Cord 812 eventually made it to Sarlat as well, and joined the Hollywood diorama, which along with the Cord L-29, featured a James Dean dummy behind the wheel. Unfortunately, Sarlat was also the place where the cylinder heads of the Cord were stolen. However, replacement parts have been in the boot of this wonderfully preserved Cord (which is now parked at Château de Sanxet) for quite some time.

1941-48 Lincoln Continental

In 1922 Henry Ford acquired the Lincoln company (which had been founded five years earlier by Henry M Leland), and henceforth, used the name for Ford's luxury division. His son Edsel, who had been at the helm of the Ford Motor Company as its president since 1919, loved to travel to Europe and visited the Continent frequently. After one of those trips, he asked designer and engineer Eugene T Gregorie to design an European-style car for him. The most striking feature of this Continental, which was based on a Lincoln Zephyr, was the vertically positioned, covered spare wheel on the boot (trunk) of the car. The term 'Continental Kit' was born and became synonymous with this feature. In late 1938, Edsel drove the finished cabriolet to Florida, where he was holidaying. In no time, he received 200 firm orders for the model. Henry Ford's initial scepticism dissolved and, as soon as Edsel returned from his vacation, the company started planning series production of both the cabriolet and the coupé. A total of 5322 Continentals were made up to 1948. The V12 had 120hp and a capacity of 4.8 litres, and in 1942 the car boasted 130hp and 5.0 litres of capacity.

Michel Dovaz owned a Lincoln Zephyr, and three Lincoln Continentals. The black coupé, with chassis number 16H.57.374, is very easy to distinguish from the other Lincolns because of its striking shark's jaw, which was typical of the first series (manufactured up to 1941). At Villemaréchal, this Continental was parked outdoors, but was one of the few vehicles that enjoyed the privilege of being placed under an open carport for some protection. Hence the body is still in decent shape overall, although the front end is rust-covered. At Sarlat, this Continental was displayed with the Panhard & Levassor in a diorama, depicting a junk shop. Now it is housed at Château de Sanxet. The gnawing rust has since been over-painted in black, although it is still clearly evident.

Dovaz's other Continentals were both from the second series (1942-48). The shark's jaw being replaced by a broad grill for this series.

Technical data: 1941 Lincoln Continental

Engine	12-cylinder V 4789cc
Bore x stroke	73.1 x 95.2mm
Compression ratio	7.2 :1
Power	120hp at 3600rpm
Top speed	78mph
W x H	203 x 162cm
Weight	1750.9kg
Wheelbase	350cm
Front track width	154cm
Rear track width	158cm
Production date	1939-41
Production number	5322 (Continental 1939-1948)
Original price	unknown

On this photo from the relocation in 1984, the Continental Kit of the 1941 Lincoln is clearly visible. (Courtesy Didier Lainé/Editions LVA)

At Villemaréchal, the light grey coupé stood next to the Lancia Dilambda in an open carport, just like the early Continental. The black cabriolet was parked in a stall with masonry walls, and a firm roof overhead.

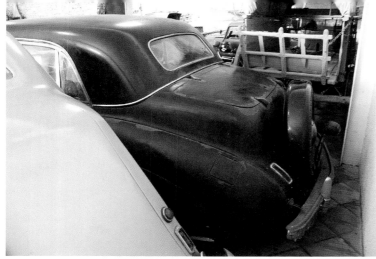

It was probably one of Dovaz's favourite cars. On the bonnet, a Ferrari sticker was visible, as Dovaz had visited Ferrari in the Italian town of Maranello, in the Lincoln at one point. Both of the second series Continentals are still owned by Dovaz today, but they are not housed at Sanxet.

At the Sarlat museum, the 1941 Continental was placed in a junk shop diorama, 1989-90.
(Courtesy Editions LVA)

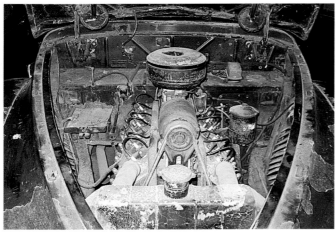

At Château de Sanxet, 2007. Note the 'shark nose'
of the first series, and the repainted rusted areas.
(Hottendorff/op de Weegh)

Technical data:
1942-48 Lincoln Continental

Engine .. ..12-cylinder V 5000cc
Bore x stroke. .. ..74.6 x 95.2mm
Compression ratio .. ...7.2 :1
Power .. ..130hp at 3600rpm
Top speed .. ..unknown
L x W x H .. ..542.3 x 188 x 165cm
Weight.. .. ..1950kg
Wheelbase.. .. ..313cm
Front track width.. .. ..148cm
Rear track width.. .. ..152cm
Production date 1942-48
Production number. .. .5322 (Continental
                                        1939-1948)
Original price .. ..unknown

A comparable second series Continental cabriolet,
which lost the 'shark nose' of the first series.
(Courtesy J Michael Jordan)

The second series Continental coupé (1942-48)
above the first series coupé (1941), loaded on one of
the relocation trucks, 1984.
(Courtesy Didier Lainé/Editions LVA)

1962-65 Rolls-Royce Silver Cloud III

In 1906, engineer Frederick Henry Royce, and businessman Sir Charles Rolls founded the Rolls-Royce Company in Manchester. The Silver Cloud model was introduced in 1955 and was succeeded by the Silver Cloud II, then in 1962 by the Silver Cloud III. The latter, identified by double headlights, was produced up to 1965, with total production reaching 2809. Of these, 2434 were made with factory bodies. The Silver Cloud III was one of the last Rolls-Royce models ever made, that involved coachbuilders, because the body and the chassis were produced separately. Various sources rated the power of the 6.2-litre V8 engine between 178 and 240hp.

Technical data:
Rolls-Royce Silver Cloud III

Engine .. ..8-cylinder V 6230cc
Bore x stroke. .. ..104 x 91mm
Compression ratio 9.0:1
Power .. ..240hp at 4600rpm
Top speed 106mph
L x W x H .. ..538 x 190 x 157cm
Weight 2000kg
Wheelbase .. ..312cm (example)
Front track width. .. .. .147cm
Rear track width.. .. .. .152cm
Production date 1962-65
Production number. .. .2434
Original price .. ..unknown

At Sanxet, the Rolls-Royce is placed amidst a pile of junk, with a canoe on its roof.
(Hottendorff/op de Weegh)

The interior of the Silver Cloud III is in poor condition at Sanxet, 2007. (Hottendorff/op de Weegh)

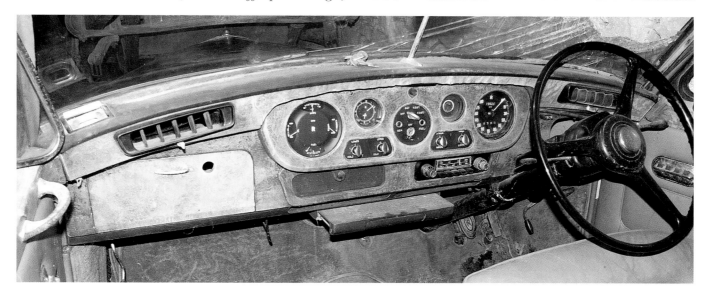

Michel Dovaz owned a Silver Cloud III with a factory body. The dented vehicle must have been in an accident, as the rear right door is missing, and the windshield has a huge hole in it. Covered with a piece of corrugated sheet metal, and situated near the entrance, it was probably one of the last cars to arrive at Villemaréchal. The presentation at Sarlat, where it was displayed as the home of an intellectual hobo, who was reading classical literature, while lounging on the backseat of the car, was definitely memorable.

At Sanxet, the Rolls-Royce is now parked in a corner, and completely blocked in by other objects. A canoe has been placed on its roof, certainly not a typical setting for a Rolls.

It's a little known fact that Michel Dovaz did in fact own a second Silver Cloud III, which was still in excellent condition in 1983. Dovaz had it sitting idly in a dry garage, because it used too much fuel. He still owns this Rolls-Royce today.

1952 Bentley R Type Hooper 'Empress Saloon'
Chassis number B114.RT

Built between 1952 and 1955, the Bentley R Type differed from its predecessor Mk VI, especially because of its longer chassis, and larger trunk. A standard steel factory body was available for this model as well, and 2038 examples of the 2528 R Types manufactured had this type of body.

In addition to the Mk VI, which is described below, Michel Dovaz had a Bentley R Type with chassis number B114.RT. The vehicle is paired with a rare Empress Saloon body made by Hooper – and is one of only 41 R Types paired with a Hooper body. The chassis was delivered to Hooper in September 1952. The first owner was Francis Guyot, who sold the Bentley to a proprietor named Wanderer (France) in 1963. The R Type is unrestored and yet so excellently preserved that it probably only spent a short time at Villemaréchal. Pictures taken of the move to the South of France prove that it was actually there at one time. The vehicle was never displayed at Sarlat, and is now housed at Sanxet.

Technical data:
Bentley R Type

Engine	6-cylinder in-line 4566cc (example)
Bore x stroke	92 x 114mm
Compression ratio	6.4:1
Power	150hp at 4500rpm
Top speed	106mph
L x W x H	512 x 175 x 170cm
Weight	1820kg
Wheelbase	305cm
Front track width	143cm
Rear track width	147cm
Production date	1952-55
Production number	2528
Original price	unknown

The Bentley R Type 'Hooper Empress Saloon,' here at Sanxet, shows an elegantly curved rear, 2007. (Hottendorff/op de Weegh)

1962-68 Alfa Romeo 2600 Sprint Bertone
Chassis number AR825930

The Alfa Romeo 2600 was launched at the Geneva Motor Show in 1962. Because of its high price and because it actually looked like its predecessor model 2300 except for a minor facelift, only about 11,500 of these cars were sold up to 1968. The 4-seater Sprint coupé, which was built by Bertone based on a concept developed by chief designer Giorgetto Giugiaro, contributed a total of close to 7000 sales to this figure. In the Sprint, the 2.6-litre, 6-cylinder, in-line engine developed 145hp.

The 2600 Sprint Bertone owned by Michel Dovaz, was only spotted at the Château de Sanxet, and was not seen at Villemaréchal and Sarlat. Dovaz did not buy the car until after the mid-1980s. It remains unrestored, and is still in excellent condition.

Technical data:
Alfa Romeo 2600 Sprint Bertone

Engine	6-cylinder in-line 2584cc
Bore x stroke	83 x 79.6mm
Compression ratio	9.0:1
Power	145hp at 5900rpm
Top speed	124mph
L x W x H	458 x 171 x 138cm
Weight	1340kg
Wheelbase	258cm
Front track width	140cm
Rear track width	137cm
Production date	1962-68
Production number	6999
Original price	unknown

The Alfa Romeo 2600 Sprint Bertone at Château de Sanxet, 2007. The car wasn't acquired by Michel Dovaz until the mid '80s.
(Hottendorff/op de Weegh)

1948-51 Tatra 600 Tatraplan
Chassis number 75.466

The roots of the Tatra Company go back to an establishment that made carriages and rolling stock in Czechoslovakia, from 1850. In 1897, it began making cars, initially under the Nesselsdorf name and, as of 1919, under the Tatra brand. The era of streamlined cars at Tatra began in 1933 with the Tatra T77 designed by Hans Ledwinka and Erich Übelacker. Models 77a, T87 and T97 were based on the same design principle. The monocoque all-steel body of the postwar model T600 Tatraplan, perfected the streamlined design of its predecessors, and offered even more room and comfort for up to six people, although the car was lightweight and fuel-efficient. The air-cooled flat-four engine developed 52hp from 2-litres capacity. The company produced 6342 Tatraplans from 1948 to 1952. About a third of them were exported – some of them to the West – so the car was a real foreign currency earner for

Czechoslovakia. In 1951, the production lines were relocated to Skoda in Mladá Bolesla, and fell victim to corporate cutbacks the following year. Tatra still makes lorries today and continued to assemble luxury cars until 1999.

Michel Dovaz's Tatra T600 Tatraplan was incorrectly identified as an 8-cylinder Tatra 97 in both books [1, 2]. The vehicle was made no later than 1951, which is evident from the pointed rear engine cowling and the small rear windows. At Villemaréchal the Tatra had a Swiss licence plate and was probably one of the 153 cars that were exported to Switzerland. The Tatraplan was parked outside at Villemaréchal, and was left exposed to the elements, covered only by a torn tarpaulin, with some tyres holding it in place. When the T600 was moved to the South of France, it had already sustained substantial damage. The interior was in a particularly pitiful state. However, the display at Sarlat attracted a lot of attention; the Tatraplan was presented as an oversized reptile in a desert scene, featuring a dune, water hole and live(!) iguanas. This vehicle, too, eventually made its way to Bertrand de Passemar. The fact

The Tatraplan in Villemaréchal during the relocation, together with a Panhard Dyna X in the foreground, 1984. (Courtesy Didier Lainé/Editions LVA)

The Tatra on one of the relocation trucks, 1984. (Courtesy Didier Lainé/Editions LVA)

Technical data:
Tatra 600 Tatraplan

Engine .. .. .4-cylinder flat 1950cc
Bore x stroke. .. ..85 x 86mm
Compression ratio.. .. ..6.0:1
Power .. .. .52hp at 4000rpm
Top speed .. .. .90mph
L x W x H .. ..454 x 167 x 152cm
Weight.. .. ..1200kg
Wheelbase .. .. .270cm
Front track width. .. .. .130cm
Rear track width.. .. .. .130cm
Production date 1948-52
Production number. .. .6342
Original price .. .. .unknown

that the T600 was in such a miserable state meant it was kept in an ancient barn, away from the main exhibition, so most visitors didn't see it. At Sanxet, the Tatra, with automotive parts, tools and some other classic cars (a Panhard PL17, Citroën Dyane and three 2CV) as its only companions, continues to gather dust. Completely unintentionally, the Tatraplan still looks exactly like the 'sleeping beauties' did back in the '80s, when they became world famous.

2007. Even inside, the Tatraplan reflects the atmosphere of Villemaréchal in 1983. (Hottendorff/op de Weegh)

In Sarlat the Tatraplan was on display in a desert scene, together with live reptiles, 1989-90. (Courtesy Editions LVA)

*At Sanxet the Tatra is placed in a
real 'barn find' scene, 2007.
(Hottendorff/op de Weegh)*

Rear of the Tatra with the distinctive fin, 2007. (Hottendorff/op de Weegh)

Class beats volume

ରେଡ଼ୁ

Regardless of the criteria one might use to structure a comprehensive collection of a variety of cars, there will always be a few that do not really fit into any of the chosen categories. The vehicles covered in this chapter are neither Bugattis nor Lancias, and certainly not Italian sports cars. They cannot be viewed at the Château de Sanxet. Nonetheless, they do have one thing in common; no matter whether they gained acclaim in their day and age, or not, they are now all coveted and rare classic cars – or simply put, cars that have a lot of class.

1951 Aston Martin DB2

Chassis number LML/50/85

In 1947, tractor manufacturer David Brown acquired Aston Martin, a company established in 1914. The models made after the takeover were marked with his initials DB. However, the DB1, which began production in 1948, only did so unofficially. The two-seater DB2, which appeared on the market in

The Aston Martin DB2 (#LML/50/85) with race number 7, next to one of the Lotus Elites in Sarlat, 1989-90. (Courtesy Dominique Delcros Archive)

In 1992 the Aston Martin was newly primed, but otherwise unrestored.
(Courtesy John Chamberlain Archive)

Technical data:
Aston Martin DB2

Engine	.6-cylinder in-line 2580cc (example)
Bore x stroke.	.78 x 90mm
Compression ratio	.6.5:1
Power	.125hp
Top speed	.110mph
L x W x H	.413 x 170 x 136cm
Weight..	.1118kg
Wheelbase..	.250.0cm
Front track width.	.137.2cm
Rear track width..	.137.2cm
Production date	.1950-53
Production number. ..	.411
Original price	.unknown

1950, boasted a newly developed 6-cylinder in-line engine, developing 105hp from 2.6 litres of capacity. The very same year, two DB2s secured the top two placements in their class at Le Mans. A second engine option that developed 125hp, became available in early 1951. By 1953, exactly 411 Aston Martin DB2s had been manufactured.

In the *Sleeping Beauties* books [1, 2], the two Aston Martin DB2s from the Dovaz collection were incorrectly identified as the 2+2-seater successor model DB2/4. The DB2 with chassis number LML/50/85 was delivered to Jean Michaud from Paris, by Aston Martin importer Majestic Autos, on December 20, 1951. Michaud drove the DB2 in France, and in his second country of residence, Switzerland. In February 1964, he sold the car to Michel Dovaz, who initially used it in Switzerland, and ultimately brought it to his property at Villemaréchal. This DB2 was displayed at Sarlat,

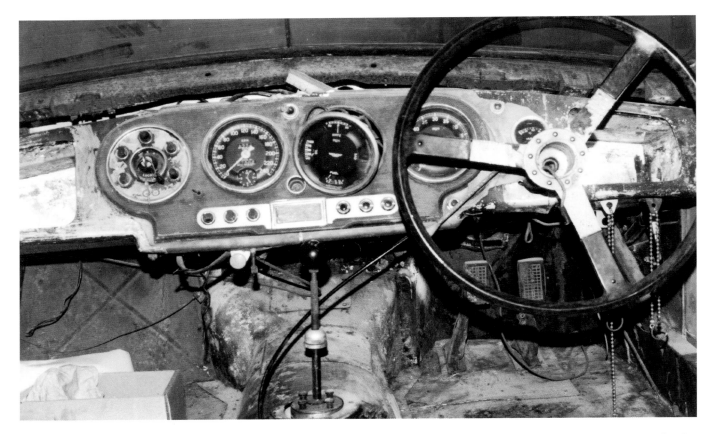

The condition of the DB2 in 1992. (Courtesy John Chamberlain Archive)

along with the two Lotus Elites, in a racing scene. After the museum was shut down, the Aston changed hands in 1990, when ownership was transferred to Thierry Giovannoni, who in turn sold the car to A Schlessinger in 1991. In 1992, the Aston Martin was still complete, and in a light-coloured primer. Schlessinger sold it to Lauren Mercier in this condition in March 1997. In 2007 it was once again offered for sale at the Eric Pérou dealership in Tours (F), albeit in a much worse condition. By then, the DB2 had been stripped of parts for use in the restoration of another Aston Martin. What

Unrestored but still complete, 1997. (Courtesy Dominique Delcros Archive)

In 2007 the car was dismantled and stripped of many parts. (Courtesy Dominique Delcros Archive)

makes this car unique, is that it was apparently converted for racing at an early stage. In addition to a supplementary air intake on the side of the bonnet, it had an additional oil cooler, a smaller alternator, and the front disc brakes of a later model DB2/4 Mk III. Unfortunately, all of these special parts have since been removed. The only feature that still identifies the car is the professionally installed air intake. On the right door, the car boasts a sign inscribed 'Ecurie Ecosse', which is the name of a successful Scottish racing team. The exact relationship of this Aston Martin with the Ecurie Ecosse team remains a mystery.

1952 Aston Martin DB2
Chassis number LML/50/177

The second Aston Martin DB2 in the Dovaz collection, which had the chassis number LML/50/177, was delivered to Papeteries Bourceer in Docelles (F) on December 10, 1952. Other owners included, R Cuny from Docelles, Commander RC Fletcher, from the US Embassy in Paris and, as of 1960, Thierry Jacques Vincens, from Paris. According to unconfirmed rumours, the car was also owned by racing car driver, DaSilva Ramos, at one point.

At Villemaréchal, this DB2 was housed in a dry barn, along with the two Alfa Romeo 6C 2500 cabriolets. After the Musée de Sarlat closed, the DB2 was transferred to Thierry Giovannoni. He recalls that he later sold the car to an Englishman.

During the relocation, 1984.
(Courtesy Didier Lainé/Editions LVA)

In the years that followed, the DB2 was offered for sale at various dealerships, first at GTC (Jean Guikas) in Marseille (F) and in 1996 for about €17,000 at Philippe Dutreux, Lille (F). Subsequently, it was also

The Aston Martin DB2 (#LML/50/177) in the 'Garage Scene' of the Sarlat museum, 1989-90.
(Courtesy Edmund Nankivell)

up for grabs at Bruno Vendiesse in Lille. In 1996, the DB2 was still unrestored and rusty, but complete, and certainly in a good enough condition for a successful renovation. The old Paris licence plate, 5369-HE-75, was also still inside the vehicle. Photos from 1996 reveal a few interesting details. The car was originally sprayed blue, with a matching interior and was painted silver grey later. This is confirmed by the factory documents. Other unique features were a top-aligned right side wiper and an elementary rear bench seat. Both are not normally found in a DB2. The whereabouts, and condition of this DB2 are currently not known.

Below and overleaf: At dealer Philippe Dutreux in Lille, 1996. (Courtesy Dominique Delcros Archive)

Technical data:
Aston Martin DB2

Engine .. ..6-cylinder in-line 2580cc
................................(example)
Bore x stroke. .. ..78 x 90mm
Compression ratio 6.5:1
Power 125hp
Top speed 110mph
L x W x H .. ..413 x 170 x 136cm
Weight 1118kg
Wheelbase 250.0cm
Front track width.. .. ..137.2cm
Rear track width 137.2cm
Production date 1950-53
Production number. .. .411
Original price .. ..unknown

1946-52 Bentley Mark VI

Bentley, a British enterprise, was founded by Walter Owen Bentley in 1919. Ridiculed by competitor Ettore Bugatti, as "... the fastest lorries in the world," the Bentleys, despite their sturdy build, won Le Mans, and other races, during the period 1927-30. The Bentley Mark VI was the first postwar model to be built between 1946 and 1952. The 6-cylinder, in-line engine of the Mk VI initially developed about 130hp from 4.3 litres, which was boosted to about 150hp from 4.6 litres in 1951. Rolls-Royce, of which Bentley became a division in 1931, offered its first standard body with the Mk VI. This standard steel body yielded a production total of 4190, making it highly successful, compared to the total of 1012 coachbuilt bodies.

Michel Dovaz owned a Bentley Mk VI standard steel, which stood in a damp barn at Villemaréchal in 1983, along with the Panhard & Levassor Dynamic, and the previously described Bentley R Type. Hence, the car was in bad condition, and was not displayed at Sarlat. Once it had been sold by Dovaz, it vanished from the scene.

Technical data: Bentley Mk VI standard steel body	
Engine	6-cylinder in-line 4257cc (example)
Bore x stroke	88.9 x 114.3mm
Compression ratio	6.4:1
Power	130hp
Top speed	94mph
L x W x H	487.7 x 175.3 x 163.8cm
Weight	1850kg
Wheelbase	304.8cm
Front track width	144.1cm
Rear track width	148.9cm
Production date	1946-52
Production number	5202
Original price	unknown

A comparable Mark VI. (Courtesy Nanno Kroen/www.otografie.nl)

The Dovaz Bentley Mark VI in Villemaréchal, circa 1983. (Courtesy La France Interdite[3]/via Gilles Delannoy)

1934-36 De Soto airflow

The US automotive make DeSoto was created in 1928 by Walter P Chrysler, who assigned it to the mid-price range of the Chrysler Group. The model designation DeSoto Airflow made its first appearance in 1934, when the streamlined Chrysler Airflow body was also offered, paired with the shorter DeSoto chassis. The Airflow with its 4-litre, V6 engine developing 100hp was a slow seller up until the series was dropped in 1936.

Michel Dovaz also owned a DeSoto Airflow. Unfortunately, we do not have a single photo of this car, and do not know whether it has ever has been in Villemaréchal. It was Michel Dovaz who told us of its existence, and who recalls that he probably sold it to someone from Canada.

Technical data:
De Soto Airflow

Engine .. .. .6-cylinder V 3958cc
Bore x stroke . .. . .85.7 x 114.3cm
Compression ratio 6.2:1
Power .. .. .100hp at 3400rpm
Top speed 87mph
L x W x H .. .. .491.8 x 183.5 x 171.0cm
Weight .. .. .1532kg
Wheelbase .. .. .292cm
Front track width. .. .. .unknown
Rear track width .. .. .. .unknown
Production date 1934-36
Production number. .. .Circa 26,000
Original price .. ..unknown

Advertising flyer for the De Soto Airflow, dated from 1935. (Courtesy Louwman Collection)

1937 Graham Supercharger 116

Graham-Paige was a company that emerged when brothers Joseph, Robert and Ray Graham acquired the Paige-Detroit Motor Company in 1927. The brothers dropped the Paige name completely in 1930, and subsequently sold all of their cars under the Graham name.

In 1934, Graham became the first US car manufacturer to offer an affordable car with a supercharger. Previously, this technology had been used only by luxury car manufacturers such as Stutz and Duesenberg. The 1936/37 models were based on the Reo Flying Cloud body, which was manufactured under licence. The 3.3-litre, 6-cylinder, in-line engine of the Supercharger 116 developed 106hp, thanks to the supercharger. Although Graham gave up car production in 1940, after numerous setbacks, it retained the record for the most supercharger-equipped cars ever made, up until the 1990s. Today,

Technical data:
Graham Supercharger 116

Engine	.6-cylinder in-line 3263cc
Bore x stroke.	.82.5 x 101.6mm
Compression ratio	.7.0:1
Power	.106hp at 4000rpm
Top speed	.80mph
L x W x H	.500.4 x 190.5 x 167.6cm
Weight..	.1500kg
Wheelbase..	.294.6cm
Front track width.	.144.1cm
Rear track width..	.155.6cm
Production date	.1937
Production number. ..	.5551
Original price	.unknown

the company has diversified into other activities, and is, among other things, the operator of New York's Madison Square Garden.

In 1983, at Villemaréchal, Michel Dovaz's Graham Supercharger 116 was parked outside, in a group with 15 other vehicles. Although the car was covered with tarpaulins, it was in a bad condition, and, due to the extent of the rust, not even its colour could be identified. The interior looked just as devastated; soiled, covered in cobwebs and rust. Nonetheless, the Graham exuded a particularly unique charisma. The vehicle was not displayed at Sarlat, and is still owned by Michel Dovaz.

The Graham Supercharger 116, during relocation to southern France, 1984.
(Courtesy Didier Lainé/Editions LVA)

1951-54 Hotchkiss Grégoire

In 1867, American Benjamin B Hotchkiss founded the French Hotchkiss company to manufacture weapons. Around the turn of the century, the company became involved in the booming automotive sector, rolling out its first car in 1903.

Hotchkiss shut down his civil car production in 1954, shortly after the company had acquired Delahaye a competitor, and continued to focus on the manufacture of military vehicles. The last civil car made was the 1951 Hotchkiss Grégoire, a co-production with automotive pioneer Jean Albert Grégoire, who designed this lightweight front-wheel-drive saloon with its 2.2-litre, flat-four engine developing 71hp. However, the complex technology drove up manufacturing costs, to the point that the sale price was no longer competitive. After just 247 cars had been made, production ceased in 1954.

Michel Dovaz owned two Hotchkiss Grégoires. One of the two was still in relatively good condition in 1983, and was parked under an open carport at Villemaréchal, next to two Lincoln Continentals and the two pre-war Lancias. The second Hotchkiss

was parked outside without any protection, and was in much worse condition. Large parts of its front (mudguards, radiator, and possibly the engine) were already missing at the time. The two Hotchkiss Grégoires were passed on to a friend of Michel Dovaz in 1990, but it's a mystery what happened to them after that.

Technical data: Hotchkiss Grégoire	
Engine	4-cylinder flat 2188cc
Bore x stroke	86 x 90mm
Compression ratio	6.5:1
Power	71hp at 4000rpm
Top speed	95mph
L x W x H	419.1 x 129.5 x 137.2cm
Weight	1080kg
Wheelbase	251.5cm
Front track width	144cm
Rear track width	132cm
Production date	1951-54
Production number	247
Original price	unknown

The first Hotchkiss Grégoire during the relocation, 1984. (Courtesy Didier Lainé/Editions LVA)

The second, incomplete Hotchkiss Grégoire on one of the relocation trucks, 1984. (Courtesy Didier Lainé/Editions LVA)

1964-68 Jaguar E-type 4.2 Cabriolet

The Jaguar E-type is probably one of the most desirable sports cars of the '60s and '70s. Available as both a coupé and cabriolet, three series totalling more than 70,000 units were made between 1961 and 1974.

The cabriolet in the Dovaz collection stemmed from the first series, which is evident from the rear lights located above the bumper. Combined with the 4.2 designation, the manufacturing period can be narrowed down to the period from 1964-68. The engine is a 4.2-litre six-cylinder in-line developing 265hp. At Villemaréchal, the car had been sitting outside, under fruit trees, but it is no longer in Dovaz's possession. Without the chassis number, finding the Jaguar appears to be virtually impossible, due to the large number produced.

Technical data:
Jaguar E-type 4.2 Cabriolet series 1

Engine	.6-cylinder in-line 4235cc
Bore x stroke	.92 x 106mm
Compression ratio	.8.0:1
Power	.265hp at 5400rpm
Top speed	.149mph
L x W x H	.445 x 166 x 122cm
Weight	.1240kg
Wheelbase	.244cm
Front track width	.127cm
Rear track width	.127cm
Production date	.1964-68 (4.2 series 1)
Production number . ..	.9550 (4.2 Cabriolet)
Original price	.unknown

Jaguar E-type, this is a comparable first series car to the Dovaz model. (Courtesy Tim Fritz)

1942-48 Lincoln Zephyr Club Coupe

The Zephyr, which was sold for a lower price than the other models in the luxury Lincoln range, represented a breakthrough for this make. When the Zephyr was launched in 1935, it was in tune with the spirit of the times. The global economic crisis had been overcome and people wanted to – and could – afford luxuries again. Designer John Tjaarda's ultra-modern streamlined design also coincided with the latest American tastes. Between 1936 and 1948, the car was built with various body styles: saloons, coupés and cabriolets. The V12 of the 1942-48 Zephyr increased the power to 120hp from 4.8 litres, or 130hp from 5.0 litres of capacity. As of 1939, the Zephyr also formed the basis of the Lincoln Continental and shared material design parameters with the latter; the front end, for instance.

We initially thought the Lincoln Zephyr in the Michel Dovaz collection was a fourth Continental. Most photos show the car from the front, and from this perspective, it is hard to distinguish between a Continental and a Zephyr. The characteristic that ultimately gave the car away was the slightly raised bonnet line of the Zephyr. It would have been much easier to identify the car from the back, as it did

not have a covered spare wheel (also known as a Continental Kit). A photo of the transporter that moved the cars to the South of France, which was published later, shows the Zephyr from the side, and reveals the exact body style to be a so-called 5 Window Coupé or Club Coupé. This was another car, that Michel Dovaz left outside at Villemaréchal. He recalls that the Zephyr was never sold, but that it simply deteriorated.

Technical data:
Lincoln Zephyr Club Coupé

Engine	V12-cylinder 5000cc (example)
Bore x stroke	74.6 x 95.2cm
Compression ratio	7.2:1
Displacement	130hp at 3600rpm
Top speed	unknown
L x W x H	unknown
Weight	1730kg
Wheelbase	317.5cm
Front track widthq	unknown
Rear track width	unknown
Production date	1942-48
Production number	253 (Club Coupé, 1942)
Original price	unknown

Lincoln Zephyr Club Coupé. This is a comparable car from 1942-48 to the Dovaz model. (Courtesy M Tyler Mathis)

1954-57 Sunbeam Mk III

For a long time, the only evidence of the existence of this car was a single photo of the rear of the car, overgrown with vegetation. In the book *Sleeping Beauties*[2], the saloon was identified as a 1947 Nash Ambassador, however, Michel Dovaz confirmed that he had never owned a Nash. Our research on the Internet, during which we compared photos of innumerable cars, ultimately led us to the Sunbeam Company. Later we saw a movie made at Villemaréchal in about 1965, which confirmed the identification of the Sunbeam Mk III. The Sunbeam brand was established in 1888 by John Marston, in Wolverhampton, England. It manufactured its first car in 1901. As a virtually unchanged successor to the Sunbeam Talbot 90, the Sunbeam Mk III was launched in 1954. By 1957, about 2250 units had been built. The 2.2-litre, 4-cylinder in-line engine developed 80hp.

At Villemaréchal, the Sunbeam Mk III owned by Michel Dovaz stood in the open without any protection, and was in a very bad condition. The fate of this car remains a mystery, and the odds on its current existence are very slim indeed.

Technical data: Sunbeam Mk III

Engine	4-cylinder in-line 2267cc
Bore x stroke	81 x 110mm
Compression ratio	7.5:1
Power	80hp at 4200rpm
Top speed	94mph
L x W x H	425.5 x 158.8 x 149.9cm
Weight	1321kg
Wheelbase	247.7cm
Front track width	128.3cm
Rear track width	128.3cm
Production date	1954-57
Production number	Circa 2,250
Original price	£1191 (1955)

The Sunbeam Mk III in Villemaréchal, 1964-65. (Courtesy Michel Pfau)

Sunbeam Talbot 90. This is a rear view of a comparable car. (Courtesy Rick Jones/www.oldclassiccar.co.uk)

'Pas important' – the offspring of mass-production

❧

Not only did Michel Dovaz have a love of expensive, luxurious and rare cars, but even mass-produced vehicles triggered his interest, and became part of his collection. Although this can be partially attributed to the fact that even someone like Michel Dovaz needed a car in which to do his shopping (especially for bulky car parts), or to tow a classic 1930s car that had broken down somewhere. Nevertheless, even these 'bread-and-butter' cars had their place at Villemaréchal, and many of them were eventually moved some 650km, to the South of France.

The fate of the Chevy is unknown. If it still exists, its identification would be next to impossible, due to the large volume of cars produced.

Comparable 1956 Chevrolet. (Courtesy Vic Brincat)

1956 Chevrolet Station Wagon

Which year most American cars were made is relatively easy to determine, given that the manufacturers usually updated their models on an annual basis. Michel Dovaz's Chevrolet Station Wagon dates back to 1956, which is evident from its grille. The lack of the 'V' beneath the grille emblem indicates that this is not a V8, but rather the 3.8-litre, 6-cylinder, in-line engine, developing 140hp. The station wagon was available in four different versions: the Handyman (2-door), the Townsman (4-door, 6-seater) or the Beauville (4-door, 9-seater). Of these three, a total of around 180,000 were made in 1956. The fourth model, which we can exclude with certainty, is the sporty Nomad which, unlike Dovaz's Chevy, had an elegantly inclined B-post.

Technical data: Chevrolet Station Wagon

Engine . . .. .6-cylinder in-line 3850cc
Bore x stroke. .. .. .. .90.4 x 100mm
Compression ratio 8.0:1
Power . . .. .140hp at 4200rpm
Top speed . .. . .unknown
L x W x H . .. . .510 x 189 x 150cm
Weight 1610kg
Wheelbase 292cm
Front track width. .. .. .149cm
Rear track width.. .. .. .149cm
Production date . .. .. .1956
Production number. .. .Circa 180,000 (1956)
Original price . .. . .unknown

1947-88 Citroën 2CV

In 1983, Michel Dovaz still had two Citroën 2CVs in his possession. One of them had the modern bonnet (as of 1960). The second, a light blue car, was probably older, given that the third side window (as of 1956) was missing. Both were parked outside near the entrance at Villemaréchal. Dovaz apparently had used them for day-to-day driving on occasions. A video, dating back to circa 1964 also shows a 2CV van. None of these three cars exist today. However, two photos taken during the move show the blue 2CV, ready to be loaded, standing between the two Aston Martins. In another picture, it can even be seen on the transporter. Michel Dovaz did not discriminate against his cars, based on their status.

Technical data:
Citroën 2CV

Engine	.2-cylinder flat 425cc (example)
Bore x stroke	.66 x 62mm
Compression ratio	.7.5:1
Power	.18hp at 5000rpm
Top speed	.59mph
L x W x H	.386 x 148 x 160cm
Weight	.540kg
Wheelbase	.240cm
Front track width	.126cm
Rear track width	.126cm
Production date	.1947-88
Production number. ..	.5,000,000 plus
Original price	.unknown

A Citroën 2CV, comparable to the later Dovaz car.
(Courtesy Henrik Betnér)

The rear of the early light blue 2CV on one of the relocation trucks, 1984.
(Courtesy Didier Lainé/Editions LVA)

1947-64 Citroën H

Naturally enough, the Dovaz collection also included the most famous French van, the Citroën H. Between 1947 and 1981, the company made around 475,000 of these vehicles, with their distinct corrugated sheet metal bodies. In addition to the factory body options, independent body shops made numerous versions to suit various purposes. Used as a delivery van, fire engine, and car transporter, the H was the number one French commercial vehicle of its era.

At Villemaréchal, the Citroën H stood next to the Tatraplan in the garden. The divided windshield indicates, that the van was built before February 1964. The odds on the survival of this commercial vehicle were very slim, after the collection was sold.

A Citroën H. This split windscreen model predates 1964 and is similar to the Dovaz van. (Courtesy Cédric Billequé)

Technical data:
Citroën H

Engine	4-cylinder in-line 1911cc (example)
Bore x stroke	78 x 100mm
Compression ratio	6.2:1
Power	50hp at 3800rpm
Top speed	48mph
L x W x H	426 x 199 x 230cm
Weight	1400kg
Wheelbase	252cm
Front track width	163cm
Rear track width	166cm
Production date	1947-81
Production number	475,000 (1947-81)
Original price	unknown

1961-67 Ford Econoline

In 1961, Ford USA launched a series of small commercial vehicles – which are still being manufactured under the E-series, or Econoline names today. The year they first rolled off the production line, Ford sold an amazing 50,000 plus units, and the entire first series, which ceased production in 1967, yielded sales of more than 400,000.

One such Econoline stood at Villemaréchal, near the exit to the property of Michel Dovaz. The Ford was certainly not one of the most enthralling vehicles in this collection, but it gives us interesting insights into its background. Initially, we were convinced that vehicles of little value were not moved to the South of France. However, eyewitness Dorien Berteletti told us that he saw an Econoline at Château de Folmont, in 1988. There the Ford was housed in a small barn, alongside a few valuable 6C Alfas. Based on this statement, we were able to actually identify the Econoline, in a blurry video from Villemaréchal. Berteletti also reported that he found various, much more valuable vehicles, that were overgrown with lush vegetation, outside at the property. Dorien claims, that a small tree was growing in the engine compartment of a small Bugatti. The unorthodox storage of his vehicles, demonstrates that the monetary value of the cars meant very little to Dovaz.

Technical data: Ford Econoline

Engine	6-cylinder in-line 2360cc (example)
Bore x stroke	88.9 x 63.5cm
Compression ratio	unknown
Power	85hp at 4200rpm
Top speed	unknown
L	442cm
Weight	1720kg
Wheelbase	229cm
Front track width	unknown
Rear track width	unknown
Production date	1961-67
Production number	400,000 plus
Original price	unknown

A Ford Econoline. A first series vehicle, like the Dovaz model. (Courtesy David Saunders)

1946-54 Panhard Dyna X

After World War II, Panhard restarted production with the small Dyna X car. The aluminium body, which is reminiscent of baroque designs, earned the car the nickname 'Louis XV'. The Dyna X had an air-cooled, flat twin engine of 610cc to 851cc (22 to 42hp). Various versions of Dyna X were made between 1946 and 1954, amounting to a total of 55,000 units. Despite its understated look, the racing versions of the Dyna X were actually placed as class winners at Le Mans and Sebring.

In the early 1980s, a pair of almost identical Dyna Xs were standing next to the Jaguar E-type, under fruit trees in Michel Dovaz's garden. One of the two saloons was in very bad condition, because its fabric roof had been destroyed, and 'Mother Nature' had taken possession of the interior. The other one, however, didn't have a fabric roof, and was in better condition. When asked about the fate of the Dyna Xs, Dovaz just mumbles "... pourri,"

Technical data:
Panhard Dyna X

Engine	2-cylinder flat 745cc (example)
Bore x stroke	unknown
Compression ratio	7.5:1
Power	35hp at 5000rpm
Top speed	72mph
L x W x H	382 x 144 x 156cm
Weight	580kg
Wheelbase	213cm
Front track width	122cm
Rear track width	122cm
Production date	1946-54
Production number	Circa 55,000
Original price	unknown

(gone to seed). Given what he thought of their highly sensitive transmission, he is no longer very fond of these cars.

One of two Panhard Dyna Xs during the relocation to southern France, 1984. (Courtesy Didier Lainé/Editions LVA)

1972-75 Volkswagen K70

The Volkswagen K70 was originally designed as the 'little brother' of the NSU RO 80 by the NSU Motorenwerke. When the company was acquired by VW the launch of the NSU, which had already been announced, was initially cancelled. However the model was eventually rolled out as the Volkswagen K70 in 1970, after customers protested. For VW, the K70 represented a technological breakthrough. The car had a front-mounted, 4-cylinder in-line engine developing 75 to 100hp driving the front wheels, while all previous Volkswagen models had sported rear-mounted, air-cooled flat-4 engines driving the rear wheels. A total of 211,127 K70s were made up to 1975.

We would never have found out about the K70, which can be seen in a blurry video dating back to 1983 at Villemaréchal, next to the Graham Supercharger, if it hadn't been for Dovaz's remark, "Nothing important, just a four-door Volkswagen." The front view in the video exactly matches the K70 post-1972, with double headlights. The car, whose rear can be seen behind some other cars in some of the photos,[2] was only about 10 years old, and was

Technical data:
Volkswagen K70

Engine	.4-cylinder in-line 1605cc (example)
Bore x stroke.	.82 x 76mm
Compression ratio	.8.0:1
Power	.90hp at 5200rpm
Top speed	.98mph
L x W x H	.442 x 169 x 145cm
Weight	.1050kg
Wheelbase	.269cm
Front track width.	.139cm
Rear track width	.142cm
Production date	.1970-75
Production number. ..	.211,127
Original price	.unknown

probably not of any great interest to the photographer. In 1983, the K70 was casually covered with a protective tarpaulin, borrowed from the neighbouring Graham. The K70 was moved to the South of France, but its fate thereafter remains a mystery. Cars rated as unimportant by Dovaz had only a very slim chance of survival.

A Volkswagen K70, similar to the Dovaz model. (Courtesy Norbert Pipper)

149

Appendix 1: Bibliography

CRED

Villemaréchal 1983-84

[1] *Schlafende Schönheiten*, HW Hesselmann &
  H Schrader, D, 1986, Ellert&Richter
[2] *Sleeping Beauties*, HW Hesselmann &
  H Schrader, CH, 2007, Edition Olms
Magazine *Stern*, D, 01.09.1983, Gruner + Jahr
Magazine *Automobile Quarterly*, #22-2, USA, 1983
  Automobile Quarterly Inc.
Magazine *GEO*, #58, F, 12/1983, Geo
Magazine *Supercar Classics*, UK, 1984,
  FF Publishing
[3] Film *La France Interdite* / French Prohibition, F,
  1984, ATC 3000
Magazine *Autoretro*, #76, F, 12/1986, Editions LVA
Magazine *Automobile Quarterly*, #25-2, USA,
  1986, Automobile Quarterly, Inc.
Magazine *Supercar Classics*, UK, 12/1987,
  FF Publishing
Magazine *KNAC*, NL, 05/1992, KNAC

Sarlat 1989-90

Advertising flyer *Fantasmes Automobiles*, F, 1989,
  RGO.
Magazine L'Automobile, F, 08/1989, SETTF.
Magazine *Retroviseur*, #13, F, 09/1989, Editions LVA
Magazine *Supercar Classics*, UK, 10/89,]
  FF Publishing
Magazine *Autoretro*, #108, F, 1989, Editions LVA
Magazine *Markt*, D, 01/1990, VF VerlagsGmbH
Magazine *The Automobile*, UK, 02/1991,
  Enthusiast Publishing Ltd.

Auction 1993

Catalogue *Bugatti*, F, 03/1993, J-C Anaf
Magazine *Retroviseur*, #57, F, 05/1993, Editions LVA

Single cars

[4] Film *Le Crime de Monsieur Lange*, F, 1936, J Renoir
Magazine *Het Klaverblaadje*, #33, NL, 1986,
  Stichting Club Alfa Romeo Bezitters
Advertising flyer *Autochic Autochoc*, F, 1988,
  Hexagon 3
Magazine *Het Klaverblaadje*, #64, NL, 1993,
  Stichting Club Alfa Romeo Bezitters
[5] Magazine *Retroviseur*, #58, F, 06/1993, Editions LVA
Magazine *Retroviseur*, #67, F, 03/1994, Editions LVA
Magazine *TV Weekeinde*, NL, ca. 1999,
  De Telegraaf BV
Magazine *Autopassion*, #133, F, 2000,
  Michel Hommell
Une Vie pour Bugatti, Y Verdier, F, 2002, Autoedition
The Bugatti Type 57S, J Kruta & B Simon, D, 2003,
  Monsenstein & Vannerdat
Magazine *Gazoline*, F, 07/2003, Pixel Press Studio
Les 57 Sport, PY Laugier, F/CH, 2004,
  Editions Bugattibook
Magazine *La Vie de l'Auto*, F, 05/02/2004, Editions
  LVA
Magazine *Autoretro*, #278, F, 2004, Editions LVA

Various

[6] *Der Fall der Brüder Schlumpf*, F Laffon &
  E Lambert, F, 1984, Bueb & Reumaux

Appendix 2:
The sleeping beauties 1983-90

✿

#			chassis #	Villemaréchal 1983	Sarlat 1989-90	restored	last known whereabouts	pages in *Sleeping Beauties* book [2]
01	1962-68	Alfa Romeo 2600 Sprint Bertone	AR825930	no	no	no	Sanxet, F (2008)	–
02	1938	Alfa Romeo 6C 2300 B Mille Miglia Touring	815053	yes	yes	yes	USA (2008)	104, 106, 120, 152, 153
03	1948	Alfa Romeo 6C 2500 Competizione	920002	yes	yes	yes	USA (2008)	88, 89, 96
04	1943	Alfa Romeo 6C 2500 SS Cabriolet Touring	915527	yes	yes	yes	I (2007)	125, 136
05	1951	Alfa Romeo 6C 2500 SS Cabriolet Worblaufen	–	yes	no	unknown	Cote d'Azur, F (1990)	125
06	1952	Aston Martin DB2	LML50-177	yes	yes	unknown	Lille, F (1996)	125, 144
07	1951	Aston Martin DB2	LML50-85	yes	yes	no	F (2008)	22, 27, 31, 63, 71, 78, 144
08	1952	Bentley Type R Hooper Empress Saloon	B114.RT	yes	no	no	Sanxet, F (2008)	146
09	1946-52	Bentley Mk VI standard steel	–	yes	no	unknown	Villemaréchal, F (1984)	85
10	1928	Bugatti Type 44 Fiacre	44580	yes	yes	yes	F (2008)	88, 89, 121, (144), 148, 150, 155
11	1931	Bugatti Type 49 Faux Cabriolet	49410	yes	yes	yes	F (2008)	(111), 144, 148, (150), 155
12	1931	Bugatti Type 50 Landaulet	50131	yes	yes	yes	A (2008)	104-106, 127, 134, 138, 152
13	1931	Bugatti Type 50 Million-Guiet	50113	yes	yes	yes	D (2008)	74, 76, 111, (138), 145
14	1933	Bugatti Type 55 Faux Cabriolet	55233	yes	yes	yes	F (2008)	96, 97, 99, 110, 112, 133
15	1936	Bugatti Type 57 Coupé Fontana	57407 ?	yes	yes	yes	I (1996)	145, 150, (151)
16	1937	Bugatti Type 57 SC Atalante	57542sc	yes	yes	yes	D (2009)	90, 94, 120, 123
17	1935	Bugatti Type 57 Ventoux	57286	yes	yes	yes	F (2008)	97-101, 107, 112, 152
18	1937	Bugatti Type 57 C Galibier	57476	yes	yes	yes	A (2008)	(111), 113, (154)
19	1956	Chevrolet Station Wagon	–	yes	no	unknown	Villemaréchal, F (1984)	28, 32, 43
20	1960-88	Citroën 2CV	–	yes	no	unknown	Villemaréchal, F (1984)	23
21	1947-56	Citroën 2CV	–	yes	no	unknown	Villemaréchal, F (1984)	–
22	1947-64	Citroën H	–	yes	no	unknown	Villemaréchal, F (1984)	(28), (87)
23	1937	Cord 812 Supercharged Custom Berline	310132B	yes	yes	no	Sanxet, F (2008)	(97), 98, (112), 114, 143, 152

#			chassis #	Villemaréchal 1983	Sarlat 1989-90	restored	last known whereabouts	pages in *Sleeping Beauties* book [2]
24	1929	Cord L-29 Sedan	2928249	yes	yes	no	Sanxet, F (2008)	105, 108, 116, 152
25	1934-36	De Soto Airflow	–	no	no	unknown	CA (1990)	–
26	1962	Ferrari 250 GTE 2+2 Coupé Pininfarina	4227GT	yes	no	unknown	Villemaréchal, F (1984)	23, 68, 87, (144)
27	1951	Ferrari 340 America Berlinetta Ghia	0148A	yes	yes	yes	USA (2008)	34, 41, 79
28	1961-67	Ford Econoline	–	yes	no	unknown	Folmont, F (1988)	–
29	1937	Graham Supercharger 116	–	yes	no	no	Dovaz, F (2008)	29, 44-47, 68, 118, 145, 148, 155
30	1951-54	Hotchkiss Gregoire	–	yes	no	unknown	Villemaréchal, F (1984)	73, 106, (155)
31	1951-54	Hotchkiss Gregoire	–	yes	no	unknown	Villemaréchal, F (1984)	22, 26, (140), 142, 147, 154
32	1961-68	Jaguar E-type 4.2 Cabriolet	–	yes	no	unknown	Villemaréchal, F (1984)	24, 52
33	1950	Jowett Jupiter Coupé Ghia Suisse	E0SA56R	yes	yes	no	Sanxet, F (2008)	86, 88, 89, 96
34	1937-39	Lancia Astura Berline Pininfarina	–	yes	no	unknown	I (199x)	67, 139, (154)
35	1951-58	Lancia Aurelia B20 GT	–	yes	no	unknown	I (199x)	28, 40, (146)
36	1951-58	Lancia Aurelia B20 GT	–	yes	no	unknown	I (199x)	33, 38, 138, 154
37	1951-58	Lancia Aurelia B20 GT	–	yes	no	unknown	I (199x)	(67)
38	1952	Lancia Aurelia B52 Coupé Vignale	B52.1015	yes	yes	yes	NL (2008)	131, 143, 154
39	1929-35	Lancia Dilambda	–	yes	yes	unknown	I (199x)	28, 73, 87, 154
40	1957-70	Lancia Flaminia Berlina	–	yes	no	unknown	I (199x)	–
41	1957-65	Lancia Flaminia GT Coupe	–	yes	no	unknown	I (199x)	26, 28, 42, 128, 143, 152
42	1957-65	Lancia Flaminia GT Coupe	–	yes	no	unknown	I (199x)	39, (87), 145
43	1942-48	Lincoln Continental Cabriolet	–	yes	no	no	Dovaz, F (2008)	102, 151
44	1941	Lincoln Continental Coupe	16H.57.374	yes	yes	no	Sanxet, F (2008)	66, 139, (155)
45	1942-48	Lincoln Continental Coupe	–	yes	no	no	Dovaz, F (2008)	28, 58, 87, 148, (150), 155
46	1942-48	Lincoln Zephyr Club Coupe	–	yes	no	unknown	Villemaréchal, F (1984)	21, 56, 63, 64, 69, 70, 154
47	1957-62	Lotus Elite	–	yes	yes	no	Sanxet, F (2008)	72, 152
48	1957-62	Lotus Elite	1012	yes	yes	unknown	Sanxet, F (1990)	50, 70, (144), 145
49	1967	Maserati Quattroporte Race Track Fire Brigade	–	no	no	unknown	unknown	
50	1936-39	Panhard & Levassor Dynamic Coupé Major	231024 ?	yes	yes	no	Sanxet, F (2008)	84, 141, 144, 152
51	1946-54	Panhard Dyna X	–	yes	no	unknown	Villemaréchal, F (1984)	25, 48, 69, (155)
52	1946-54	Panhard Dyna X	–	yes	no	unknown	Villemaréchal, F (1984)	25, 30, 54, 61
53	1962-65	Rolls-Royce Silver Cloud III	007851 ?	yes	yes	no	Sanxet, F (2008)	23, 60, 71, 82, 121, 139
54	1962-65	Rolls-Royce Silver Cloud III	–	yes	no	no	Dovaz, F (2008)	–
55	1954	Siata 208 CS Coupé Balbo	CS074	yes	no	yes	B (2008)	97
56	1954-57	Sunbeam Mk III	–	yes	no	unknown	Villemaréchal, F (1984)	2, 36
57	1948-51	Tatra 600 Tatraplan	VC 75.466	yes	yes	no	Sanxet, F (2008)	28, 60, 62, 63, 70, 75, 149, (155)
58	1972-75	Volkswagen K70	–	yes	no	unknown	Villemaréchal, F (1984)	(29)

Appendix 3: Map of the
Dovaz property, 1983

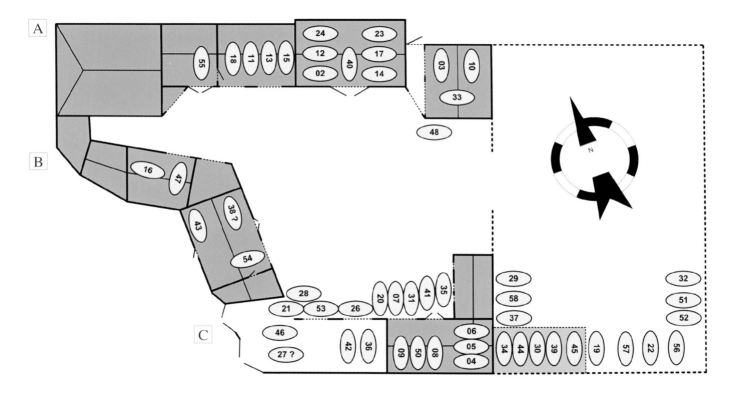

A

B

C

153

Appendix 4: GPS coordinates of the event locations

CRS8D

Former Dovaz property in Villemaréchal

Longitude   02°52'05" E
Latitude   48°16'00" N

Note: There have been no cars here since 1984.

Former museum in Sarlat

Longitude   01°13'00" E
Latitude   44°53'34" N

Note: There have been no cars here since 1990.

Château de Folmont

Longitude   01°14'07" E
Latitude   44°22'41" N

Note: There have been no cars here since 1991.

Château de Sanxet

Longitude   00°26'04" E
Latitude   44°48'21" N

www.sanxet.com
(winery and public automobile museum)

Source: www.geoportail.fr

Hardback • 25x25cm • 96 pages • 62 pictures • £14.99* UK / $24.95* USA
ISBN: 978-1-845843-46-5

Sleeping Beauties USA honours rusted and forgotten automotive treasures that have been found parked alongside the highways of America. Featuring stunning and evocative photography, this book illustrates the transient and inherent beauty of these cars.

For more info on Veloce titles, visit our website at www.veloce.co.uk • email: info@veloce.co.uk • Tel: +44(0)1305 260068
* prices subject to change, p&p extra

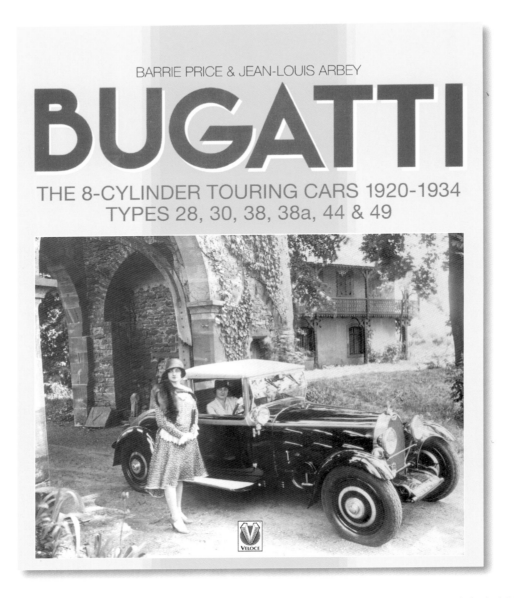

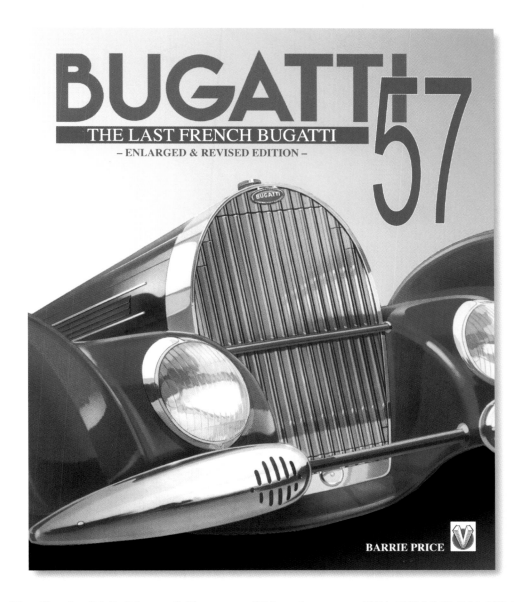

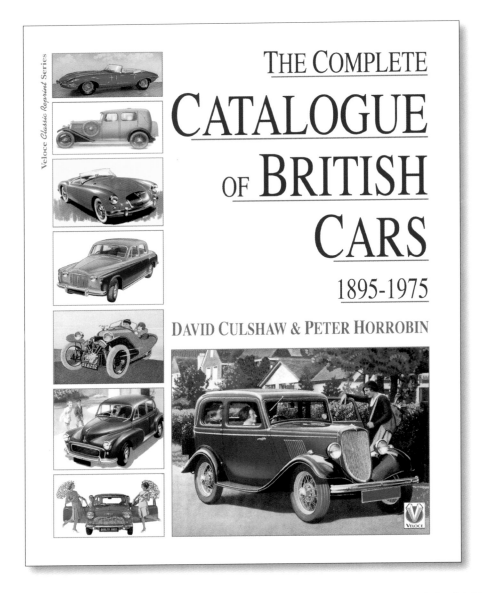

Hardback • 21.5x27.8cm • 496 pages • 1000+ b/w pictures • £30* UK / $54.95* USA
ISBN: 978-1-874105-93-0

The most comprehensive account of British cars ever published in one volume, this book presents a huge amount of information – historical as well as technical – in a way which will serve the needs of the dedicated enthusiast, automotive historian and general reader.

For more info on Veloce titles, visit our website at www.veloce.co.uk • email: info@veloce.co.uk • Tel: +44(0)1305 260068
* prices subject to change, p&p extra

$\mathcal{I}$ndex

∞☙